Darling ......,
Happy Christmas!
Enjoy the oddness of this
brilliantly random book. All my
love,
Hxxx

BRITISH
POLICE CARS
OF THE
1950s & '60s

Alan Johnson
&
Robert Berry

Nostalgia Road Publishing

CONTENTS

The **Nostalgia Road** Series ™

is produced under licence by

Nostalgia Road Publications Ltd.

Units 5 - 8, Chancel Place, Shap Road Industrial Estate,

Kendal, Cumbria, LA9 6NZ

Tel. +44 (0)1539 738832 - Fax: +44 (0)1539 730075

designed and published by

Trans-Pennine Publishing Ltd.

PO Box 10, Appleby-in-Westmorland, Cumbria, CA16 6FA

Tel. +44 (0)17683 51053 Fax. +44 (0)17683 53558

e-mail: admin@transpenninepublishing.co.uk

and printed by

Kent Valley Colour Printers Ltd.

Kendal, Cumbria - +44 (0)1539 741344

© Text: Trans-Pennine Publishing Ltd. 2006
© Photographs: As credited

Front Cover: *From the 1960s Lancashire Constabulary began using succeeding generations of the Zephyr Six models. By the 1960s the traditional black had been replaced by this white and 'Day-glo' orange scheme for motorway patrol cars.* Lancashire County Constabulary

Rear Cover Top: *Wolseley saloons had been the symbolic police patrol car for decades with a large number of police forces until the cessation of the marque. This preserved 'look-a-like' car is one of the Wolseley 6/100 models.*

Rear Cover Bottom: *Foreign-made vehicles were originally taboo in Britain, but on of the first to be tried was the Volvo 120 series Amazon estate which was used by Hampshire Constabulary; this example has recently been fully restored.* Volvo

Title Page: *This is a photograph to make anyone warm to the police force. There is almost a paternal benignity about these Irish police officers on parade with their Vauxhall Velox patrol cars.* Vauxhall Motors

This Page: *One of the most typical police cars during the period concerned was the Wolseley 6/80 model, such as this 1952 example.* Metropolitan Police

ISBN 1 903016 14 2

British Cataloguing in Publication Data

A catalogue record for this book is available from the British Library

INTRODUCTION

As every schoolboy of the 1950s and early 1960s knew, British police cars were big, black and had shiny chrome bells on their front end. These large saloon cars were reserved for elite police work, and the average 'bobby' only had a pair of black shiny boots, or maybe a pushbike if he was lucky. Television of the time showed the contrast, with programmes between the two, as *Dixon of Dock Green* and *No Hiding Place* demonstrated different aspects of policing. Then with the coming of the motorways and greater car-ownership, the face of the police motor sections changed dramatically. This was captured in another BBC TV programme called *Z Cars*, which entertained massive audiences with the thrills of life in the squad cars in the fictitious town of Newtown in Lancashire.

Despite being a good Yorkshire lad, this was compulsive viewing. From those days, actors like Brian Blessed and Stratford Johns soon became household names, whilst the white MkII Fords were soon every bit as famous. This was the first real British drama series centred on police car work, and it inspired a whole new generation.

In the years that followed I took more than a passing interest in police work, and I even passed to join the West Yorkshire force in 1974 when it looked as though my employers were about to make me redundant. However, a change of circumstances meant I got a transfer to another part of my firm's organisation. Choosing that against a new career in the police, I was accepted for the 'specials'. But once again circumstance intervened, as I was more urgently needed by the local mountain rescue team. In the years that followed I often worked with police officers in combined operations and got to admire the cars and equipment with which they worked.

This book is a record of how the police became motorised in the 1950s and 1960s, and is written by a number of contributors. Alan D. Johnson had started the manuscript back in 1998, but he sadly passed away at his Buckinghamshire home in September 2002. Much more additional material has since been supplied by interested police forces and individuals, and completed by my colleague Robert Berry to whom I am most grateful.

Alan Earnshaw   Appleby October 2006

Above: *With the ever increasing amount of cars on the road, traffic accidents were becoming far too common an occurance. Thus the importance of the introduction of speed restrictions. A police constable at the scene of a typical multi-car accident.*
Vauxhall Motors

IN AT THE START, by Alan D. Johnson

The opening of the Preston Bypass on 5th December 1958 heralded the start of a new era in road travel and the beginnings of what we now know as the national motorway network. A little ahead of this event I had been appointed as a vehicle performance evaluator for the Home Office, with special responsibility for emergency service and highway maintenance vehicles. As it was clearly recognised that the face of motoring was to change massively in the next few years, as the Conservative government of the day had decided to modernise and equip the nation's police forces to be able to combat what had been perceived as a new threat - car crime. That is not to say, the theft of automobiles (taking and driving away), but new opportunities that would be presented to organised criminals who could use fast powerful cars on the newer, better roads that the state was going to build.

Having worked in the Civil Service for ten years, by 1951 I could easily recognise that the socialist ideas of the first post-war Labour government were going to take a dramatic sea change, and it was obvious to many of us that free enterprise/trade would be at the heart of it. It was also obvious that an almost pathological hatred existed for the ideology behind nationalised transport, and that the Tories would do their best to rid themselves of the nationally-owned railways, buses and road haulage.

In the period 1948 to 1955, I had been an analyst within the British Transport Commission, and I was personally involved in supplying figures to the new Conservative Transport Minister after the General Election of 1952. With the demise of British Road Services as de-nationalisation substantially reduced the fleets, my own position was tenuous to say the least. However, I saw (and applied for) a listing for a senior officer at the General Post Office.

To my surprise I was appointed into the new job, without being ever called for an interview, and from September 1955 to the middle of 1958, I spent my time happily purchasing vehicles for the Post Master General's fleet. Yet, at the same time I maintained friendships with my former colleagues at the BTC, and one day in 1957 one of them told me that Harold McMillan (the British Prime Minister of the day) had decided that they were 'going for the railways next'. Presumably meaning that after successfully de-nationalising British Road Services, they would then turn their attention to dismantling British Railways.

"Goodness knows where it will all end" said my friend (a fervent socialist), "but I think they want to close down all the railways and build straight, wide roads on the track-beds." He added that these new roads would be called Motor Ways, but I laughed at his next statement that "they would be six lanes wide in places." I seriously doubted that he had really understood the concept of what he was then being asked to do, but now I am sure he did!

Above: *In this 1930s photograph, we see Deputy Chief Constable Gray of Renfrewshire County Constabulary with his Vauxhall Light Six, and the Vauxhall Big Six that was used for police work.* Vauxhall Motors

He explained that he had been seconded to a team that would devise a plan for this new 'Motor Way' network, and that the team would have to come up with 'figures' that showed that the development of such a network was more cost-effective than the money that was already ear-marked for railway modernisation. Another former colleague told me much the same thing, but he had the opposite task, he was to work with another 'pre-determined' plan that would show that the railway network required substantial reduction as the only way to achieve profitability.

Yet a third person, a former college friend then working at the Home Office, told me of the new ACIS Unit (Acquisition, Certification and Inspection Section) who would have the responsibility for setting new national guidelines for a purchasing policy centred around the new 'Motor Way' network. I looked in the 'listings' found the job and applied for it, but after a seemingly successful interview my section head at the GPO refused to let me go! I thought that the ACIS had obviously appointed someone else, as the job was due to commence on 1st January 1958, but at the end of my summer holiday leave in August, I returned to Ealing to find a telegram had been sent calling me for a second interview. The date of the interview was the Friday before I returned from my holiday. My wife said I should not be put off by this fact, and at 9am prompt I was on the telephone explaining the situation to the personnel officer. As a result of that call in the summer of 1958, I started in the post two weeks later and for the next 29 years I had the responsibility for determining the types of vehicles that would be suitable for use in police work, motorway maintenance, service work and so on.

Of course we never told the local authorities what they had to buy, but simply listed the kind of vehicle's that the State thought would meet the criteria and were thus put on the 'approved list'. We got to test all manner of vehicles, but the big embargo was NEVER BUY FOREIGN CARS, as we had to support the British Motor Industry at all costs, but *we could test* the overseas offerings, and we did!

Above: *When the police forces were motorised, the type of vehicles were largely dependant on the preferences of local constabulary. The British car industry at this time was quite substantial, offering a tremendous amount of choice. In the 1920s Edinburgh acquired these Alvis drop-head coupes.* Lothian and Borders Police

During the last 40-years the size of the motorway network and the volume of traffic has increased dramatically. The responsibility of policing the motorways and maintaining the safety of the travelling public falls to the officers of the Motorway Units of the various metropolitan, county or regional constabularies. But times have greatly changed since the days of the Preston By-pass, and today the general public comes under far greater scrutiny than they did back in 1958. And rightly so, for our roads are now packed with drivers, many of whom not only flout the laws designed to protect them, but do so just for the sake of expediency or simply for the fun of it. There was no national speed limit back in 1958, even the 20mph and 30mph restrictions had been lifted off commercial vehicles and buses, and speeding began to increase. Even so, our roads were not yet wide-open race tracks, and the speeds of 100mph (or the ton) that some claimed to achieve were often flights of fancy by people driving cars whose top speed was perhaps 60mph with a following wind.

With people on motorbikes it was a different tale however, and I could tell many sad tales of the efforts we had to provide the police with cars fast enough to catch speeding bikers. One poignant event I remember occurred when I was evaluating a new Riley prototype sports model with the North Riding County Constabulary in 1961, which we eventually took out on the A64 York - Scarborough road. The driver was a civilian from BMC at Cowley, and we were overtaken east of Malton by a group of 'Rockers' heading east. The Inspector sitting in the back with me decided that the pursuit would have to be made by a uniformed officer, and he made the driver swap seats with his sergeant who had been acting as an observer. Pursuit was given but it did not go on for long because, after rounding a bend we came across the all-to-frequent results of kids 'doing the ton' - a road traffic accident (RTA) with two fatalities.

Yet, there was no road rage in those days, the nearest thing you got to any kind of 'hand signal' was a salute from a roadside AA or RAC patrolman. A motorist who had broken down would as often as not find he got a helping hand from a passing police patrol car as he did from one of the motoring club mechanics, and I have even seen footsore hitchhikers and 'gentlemen of the road' being given a lift on their way by a police car in times of inclement weather. Kids on buses would wave at police cars, and policemen would wave back!

The police may have just become mobile, but they were still essentially local bobbies who had yet to become insular and remote from the communities they served! The push-bike, the noddy-bike and the Panda car were all stages in this isolation of police and community, but in the 1950s and 1960s this was not understood as being a dangerous side-effect of mobilising the police.

I said earlier that it was car crime that the police were trying to crack when it decided to mobilise the force, and that is essentially correct. Yet, as early as 1960 my office had been alerted that a primary responsibility for the police would be to prevent motoring offences. High speeds were not then illegal, there were no MoT tests, vehicle conditions were not a big concern, long driver hours were accepted as commonplace, and it was an almost social pre-requisite that almost every motorist, excursion coach driver, lorry driver or motorbiker would stop at a public house for a swift pint or two (or three or four) on the way back from a day's outing. 'One for the road' was a common saying back in the 1950s, but it was a practice that would become increasingly more dangerous as the roads became busier. So, if we weren't thinking about these issues, what did we concern ourselves with?

Well, one of the oddest matters I had to deal with was what type of vehicle we would recommend to police forces for getting dangerous road users off the new motorways. These dangerous users included horse-riders, pedal cyclists, and tractor drivers; my how things have changed! One problem was how we could remove unattended/attended cattle from the motorways and although I gave the matter some mental debate for weeks on end, I could see no solution other than herding them. That is until my ten-year-old daughter Debbie said, "Daddie, why don't you get some horse-boxes for the policemen, and then when they don't need them on the motorways they can have them for the police horses instead!"

It was indeed a time of change, and one with which I am proud to have spent my working days. In that time I certainly had some interesting experiences, testing anything from snowploughs to police cars. I like to think it was a big job played by a small insignificant team, but we always believed that what we did had real value.

Top Right: *During the infancy of motorising the police forces, cars tended to be chosen for their reliability and performance. Illustrated here is PC William Markham of the West Riding Constabulary with a Standard Nine.* Courtesy Joan Newsome

Middle Right: *Commercial vehicles played an early crucial role in the police forces, serving such diverse roles from prison vans, horse-boxes or communication systems. This is a Morris Commercial, with generator trailer.* Morris Commercial Cars

Bottom Right: *The earliest examples of motor vehicles in many police forces were the prison vans, here is one such example based on a 1934/5 Bedford chassis.* Vauxhall Motors

THE ORIGINS, by Alan D. Johnson

The word 'Police' means the arrangements made in all civilised countries to ensure that the inhabitants keep the peace and obey the law. The word also denotes the force of peace officers (or police) employed for this purpose. In attaining this goal by these officers, a great deal depends on the respect and co-operation of the general public, and these factors have always been determined by the degree of esteem in which the police are held. One of the key principles of policing in Britain has always been that the police have tried to work as part of the community. Whilst some may not agree with me, I believe this principle still holds true down to this day.

The origin of the British police lies in ancient history, for it is based on tribal customs in securing order through the medium of appointed representatives. In effect, the people always controlled the police. The Saxons brought to England a system where the people were divided into groups of ten, called 'tythings', with a tything-man as representative of each. These were then organised into larger groups, each of ten tythings, under a 'hundred-man' who was responsible to the Shire-reeve, or Sheriff of the County.

Above: *This photograph shows an impressive line up of cars in the West Riding Of Yorkshire County Constabulary during the late 1940s period. From left to right we see a Standard 14, Humber Snipe, Wolseley 14, Jaguar, Austin 16 and a Vauxhall J Type. This was a time when the main criterion for the cars was that they had to be reliable and British.* West Yorkshire Constabulary

Following the introduction of a feudal law system by the Norman's after 1066, the tything-man system changed considerably but was not wholly destroyed. In time the tything-man became the parish constable and the Shire-reeve the Justice of the Peace, to whom the parish constable was responsible. This system, had become widely established by the 17th and 18th centuries, and usually one comprised of an unarmed able-bodied man in each parish, who was appointed or elected annually to serve for a year as the parish constable. He worked (usually unpaid) in co-operation with the local Justices in maintaining order. In the towns, responsibility for policing was placed on elected groups of citizens, who in turn supplied bodies of paid men, known as 'The Watch', for guarding the gates and patrolling the streets at night.

With the coming of the Industrial Revolution and the mass migration of people from the countryside to live and work within Britain's towns and cities, came the beginnings of immense social and economic changes. In this often volatile climate, the parish constable and 'Watch' systems failed completely and the issue of law-enforcement became a serious public concern.

As conditions deteriorated, especially in the urban areas, it led to the formation of the 'New Police' and what happened in London is perhaps the very best example. As London expanded, the whole question of maintaining law and order became a matter of concern. Parliamentary committees were appointed in 1812, 1818 and 1822 to investigate the subject. Eventually in 1828 the Home Secretary, Sir Robert Peel set up his committee, which led to the Police Bill and the setting up of an organised police service in London. It is on account of Sir Robert Peel's name that the early reference to the police as 'Peelers' and later 'Bobbies' came into vogue.

In 1829 the first Metropolitan Police Act was passed and the Metropolitan Police Force was established to replace the local Watch in the London area. Yet, even within the Metropolitan Police District there still remained certain police establishments, organised during the 18th-Century, that did not yet come under the control of the Metropolitan Police Office. These included the City of London and The Bow Street Patrols, the latter were both mounted and foot, with the foot patrols being known as the 'Bow Street Runners'. Those Police Office constables, along with the Marine or River Police, were under the control of the Magistrates. However, by 1839 most of these establishments had been absorbed by the Metropolitan Police Force, but the City of London Police (set up in 1839) remained aloof and still is an independent force to this day.

Top Right: *Although the motorisation of the police forces was very advanced during the 1940s and '50s, the general public's point of view of law enforcement was by means of the constable on the beat. The lone policeman in his smart uniform with the recognisable tall helmet was a stable British institution and an unchanging way of life until the debatable success of the panda cars in the early 1960s. In the typical scene pictured here, a police constable assists the driver of a 1931 Morris saloon. Note the period AA badge on the radiator grille of this time-served car.* Avon Constabulary

Bottom Right: *Police officers had to strongly adhere to the same standards of rules and discipline as military personnel. They were inspected before going out on their beat or on patrol, so the officers, their equipment and their patrol cars were always immaculate. This was not just a duty, but was more often than not a personal sense of pride, indeed many police officers were often actually recruited from the armed forces where 'spit and polish' was the norm. A police patrol officer of the Somerset Constabulary poses proudly with his Ford Zephyr MkI saloon during a quiet moment.* Avon Constabulary

Above: *Could one of these States of Jersey officers be Jim Bergerac's grandfather? Photographed outside the police head-quarters on the Channel Island, Jersey police officers in their heavy tunics pose proudly with their Vauxhall model H. Judging by the registration number, this band of men had only 15 motorists to pursue.* Courtesy Val Nelson (Jersey Museums Service)

Most British police forces can trace their origins back to the passage of an Act of Parliament in 1835, when the Municipal Corporation Act required provincial boroughs to set up a police force. The experiences in the London area had shown that improvements through the 'New Police' system had been both significant and rapidly introduced! In many ways the Metropolitan Police became a role model for forces all over the British Isles, as well as many others in colonial lands or in other parts of the world. Scotland employed different laws, but the principle was the same.

The start of mobile policing can certainly be traced back to the Victorian-era, when both horses and horse-drawn carts were provided. The horse and carts were simple to explain, as the bulk of those used were simply kept for Police Court duties, namely the transfer of felons from police cells to court by a secured means of transport. Very few of those carts were actually used to collect a miscreant from the scene of the crime to the local police station and in most cases the 'bad lad' would be frog-marched in a pair of handcuffs from the scene of crime by a couple of burly bobbies.

In those early days, the purchase costs of horses and carts, and the ongoing upkeep for such facilities did not endear them to the local Watch Committees, and there were few luxuries for the policemen and even less for the criminals. Mounted police were not unknown, and as indicated earlier in this section, the Bow Street Police had a mounted division, as did a number of other local forces. The mounted police units were often operated on military lines, and in some parts of the British Empire these mounted units were known as Police Cavalry. It is also known that then, as now, the police often had a tendency to recruit military personnel who had just left the armed services. Such men were highly trained and well disciplined, and the majority found the ostensibly arduous police work something of a 'cushy billet' after their service in the forces.

Mounted units were used for rapid response, but more often than not their main use was for riot control; indeed, the intimidation factor of a huge horse and burly rider charging down on an unruly crowd is still a good deterrent at the start of the 21st century. However, for the majority of officers it was a case of pounding the beat, but several forces did allow their men to purchase bicycles. The more generous ones even paid them a maintenance allowance, as for example the Hampshire County Constabulary who allowed 15 shillings for the maintenance of the cycles.

On this police transport expert Steve Woodward wrote: "This allowance commenced on 1st January 1898 and was payable quarterly. The Chief Constable of the time, Major Warde later secured authority from the Standing Joint Committee for it to be increased to 30 shillings per year." However as a condition of this increase, he insisted that all cycles ridden by police officers had to be fitted with brakes. Further improvements came in 1903-4 when the Automobile Club (later the RAC) supplied red reflectors that a policeman could fit to the back of his cycle if he wanted. This was done to advertise the safety value of such devices, and is an example of what we might now call 'commercial sponsorship.'

The horse still remained the primary means of transport for senior officers, and generally each officer attaining the rank of Superintendent or above was paid an allowance to keep a horse and cart. In some forces, Inspectors were also supplied with their own transport, and this became an increasing trend as time progressed. A police driver was also supplied, and several forces actually banned senior officers from driving themselves, a trend that continued down into the days of motorised transport. The transport was supplied so that the officer could travel around the stations to inspect his men, or to travel rapidly to an incident or emergency. In such incidents it was not uncommon for the horse and cart to pick up officers from their beats en-route. As a consequence, the carts supplied to senior officers were usually four-seaters.

Top Right: *In today's world, a police car will request you to stop by showering the night with a burst of electric stanza, and drivers have to leave their car and walk back for a quiet word. Previously as with the officer of this Vauxhall 14-Six model 'J' type, they would talk to the miscreant on the roadside.* Vauxhall Motors

Middle Right: *Vauxhall motors introduced their L type Velox and Wyvern models during 1948. These were principally based on the old Ten-Four HIY and the Twelve-Four HIX models, but with new front and rear ends, also incorporating an alligator type opening bonnet. Here we see one of the 'L' series Vauxhall Velox cars of Liverpool on convoy duty.* Courtesy Tony Roche

Bottom Right: *Also in the North West, these two late examples of the Ford E83W Utilicon-are serving with the Mersey Tunnel Police. These Liverpool-registered vehicles are equipped with high-visibility warning signs.* Courtesy Tony Roche

MOTORISING THE FORCE, by Alan D. Johnson

The advent of the internal combustion engine, at the same time, was both one of the greatest innovations ever employed by the police and also one of the greatest innovations used against society. The speed with which motor vehicles could be used by the less-honest members of society in pursing nefarious activities may now seem quite obvious, but in the Edwardian era it was a threat that the public had yet to understand. Indeed, the first police cars were actually purchased with little thought to their value in policing, and were more often than not viewed as status symbols by the senior officers to whom they were allocated.

Several forces used big six-cylinder cars, like Vauxhall and Napier, but prestige cars were also employed including Rolls Royce and Bentley. In some forces however, it became an uphill struggle for even senior officers to acquire their own motorised transport (especially in Scotland and Ireland) and many had to argue with frugal police or watch committees to retain their pony and trap.

Above: *The idea of motorising the police forces was at one time seen to be a total extravagance, with only the very high ranking officers attaining this privilege. It was therefore only after World War II, with the changing structure of society and the rapid influence of the motor vehicle that police cars became a vital priority. Recalling a more leisurely time here the Chief Constable of Reading is chauffeur-driven in his Austin Tourer.*
Berkshire Constabulary

It seemed that motor vehicles for use as prison van's were more readily justified, and these vehicles became another sort of status symbol, as they appeared to demonstrate to the public at large, that justice was both swift and secure. Morris, Burford and Milnes-Daimler seem to have been popular chassis on which locally-built prison van bodies would be mounted. Even so, it would not be until after the Great War of 1914-18 that the vast majority of forces would begin serious motorisation - a process that was aided by the number of drivers and vehicles returning home after military service.

Top Right: *This view shows an impressive line-up of the Vauxhall J Type saloon cars that served in Liverpool during the 1940s.* Vauxhall Motors

Middle Right: *Here we have a brace of Morris 8 series E models, new to the West Riding force in 1941. First-hand knowledge of these cars allows me to say that their performance was limited. On seeing a hill the car would give a sigh from its 29bhp engine then just resign itself to the effort.* West Yorkshire Constabulary

Bottom Right: *With so many police officers joining the armed services during World War II, many forces suffered an acute man-power shortage. This was largely redressed by the recruitment of a large intake of female staff. The WPC crew of this 1939 West Riding Hillman Minx receive a briefing from their station sergeant, prior to leaving on patrol.* West Yorkshire Constabulary

The fact that motor vehicles improved tremendously due to the war of 1914-18 was coupled with the fact that many more men could now drive, including hundreds of policeman who had joined up at the outbreak of the hostilities. Many of the vehicles purchased by police forces after the 'Great War' were military surplus, which were offered to local authorities by the Government at heavily discounted rates. Not all of these were of British manufacture, and several cars and vans were of American origin, but the reliability of these cars and spares issues eventually gave rise to a great distrust of 'imported vehicles'.

One American firm that found a niche market for a competitively-priced new car was Ford, who sold hundreds of Model Ts to police forces all over Europe. However, by opening an assembly plant and later a manufacturing facility in England, they were able to get around many of the prejudices that other firms faced. Manufactured at Trafford Park in Manchester, the Model T Ford was cheap enough to provide to officers at the rank of Inspector with their own transport. Another American firm to make an attempt to get a foothold in the British market was the Hudson company, but with regard to British sensitivities it branded its UK-built models under the name Essex after the county in which they were assembled.

British makes all contended in the field, with Austin, Hillman, Humber, Morris, Riley, Singer, Vauxhall and Wolseley each finding their particular adherents. Commercial chassis were also purchased in significant numbers, for not only were they used for prison vans, but police-owned ambulances and fire engines as well. It is not intended to dwell on these vehicles in any length, as a) they are not police cars, and b) they are to be covered in other books within this series. However, it is important to remind the reader that, in many parts of the country, fire and ambulance services also came under the control of the Chief Constable. This situation would remain a matter of local decision until the re-formation of the fire and health services by the first socialist post-war Government in 1948!

Above: *Traditional Riley models were offered with a choice of 1.5 or 2.5-litre engines. The RMB models with the larger engine served in many forces during the 1940s and '50s; West Sussex Constabulary was just one enthusiastic user.* Sussex Constabulary

In the fullness of the account of mobile policing between the wars, we ought to make some mention on the subject of police motorcycles, as these were widely employed by some forces as a mid-way stage between push-bikes and full motorisation. However, to do full justice to the subject would take a complete book in its own right, and such a volume might one day appear in the **Nostalgia Road** series.

As we concern ourselves with police cars it is fitting to look at the one piece of legislation that brought about the greater mobility of the police forces in England & Wales, which came in the form of the Road Traffic Act of 1930. This piece of legislation changed many things on the country's roads but Section 57(4) was of particular interest to the enforcing authorities. This section stated that advances could be made from the Road Fund and used for the expenses incurred by the Police in the provision and maintenance of vehicles or equipment required for the enforcement of the said Act.

Accordingly, the Home Office stated that grants would be paid annually in advance to cover vehicles that were running 12,000 miles a year. The grants were graded to different vehicles, with £60 per annum for solo motor bicycles, £80 per annum for combination motor cycles and £120 per annum for motor cars. This paved the way for a flood of new police cars and motor cycles, and amongst the more popular were the Alvis Tourer, Austin 10 and Austin 7, Daimler 15hp, Ford V8, Lanchester 15hp, Morris 8, Morris 10, Morris Cowley and Morris Isis 18hp, Riley 9hp, Riley 'one-two' 12hp, Vauxhall Light Six, Vauxhall 15hp, and the Wolseley 2-litre. Small, fast sports cars were also purchased and examples of these included the MG Midget and the Wolseley Hornet. Even large American saloons entered some fleets such as the Ford model B.

This is by no means an exhaustive list, but it gives a flavour of what would have been seen on our roads, at a time when private car ownership was steadily growing. In 1931 (at the lowest point in the Depression) just under 160,000 new cars were licensed in Britain, but by 1938 this figure had grown to a substantial 400,000 and car ownership stood at around 2,000,000 although it long remained the preserve of the rich and middle class.

Yet with the outbreak of war in 1939, police forces found a greater and more urgent need for mobilisation, after all this was going to shortly become a time of a severe national emergency. The problems of 'threatened' enemy action were coupled with the difficulties of staff shortages as mentioned earlier. To solve the problem, women were recruited to the ranks of many police forces, and these WPCs proved themselves invaluable. This time in Britain's history also became obviously infamous as a period of severe rationing, as restrictions and 'make do and mend' became the norm, as even the most basic commodities were in extremely short supply. Fortunately several members of the public donated their own cars to their local constabularies, especially as petrol was rationed for all but the emergency services; other vehicles became dependant on gas conversion.

To say that many police forces were stretched to their limits at this time, is an understatement for not only had they to contend with the conventional peacetime crime and crime prevention, but they also had many wartime duties as well. These included the further encumbrances of bomb damage and casualties, the black market, and the black-outs with the injuries and fatalities it caused as people and cars were involved in accidents caused by the total blackness. During this time the majority of urban police officers walked the beat, but bicycles were widely used in more rural localities, as crime was on the increase. This became even more apparent after the war when rationing was only marginally lifted. In this time theft was an increasing occurrence and gangsterism started, and this was portrayed in period movie films like the classic *Brighton Rock* starring Richard Attenborough.

With an increase in more serious crimes, parts of the country had an almost American underworld existence, with an alarming increase in gang warfare. Throughout the country car-related crimes rose sharply in relation to the increasing population. Road accidents, the theft of cars and armed robberies with villains using stolen cars as get-away vehicles became widespread.

Top Right: *Radio control was one way of beating the criminal, and here we see a 1952 Vauxhall E-series provided with an additional battery to power the radio. Vauxhall introduced their new range of four- and six-cylinder cars during 1951, which were respectively known as the Wyvern and Velox . These cars were originally powered by the same engines that were fitted to the interim L series models. Later the E series received new short-stroke OHV engines during 1952. These new four-cylinder 1.5-litre for the Wyvern and six-cylinder 2.2 unit for the Velox produced more power than the previous engines. Vauxhall Motors*

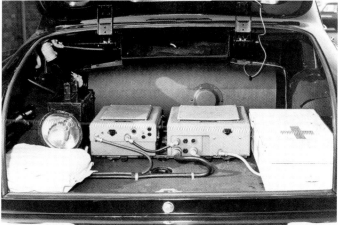

Bottom Right: *The rear view of the same Vauxhall Velox shows the equipment needed for a radio patrol car of the early-1950s. However, the extra battery for the radio could only be sited where the heater unit was fitted on ordinary saloons, and this meant cold comfort for the crews. Vauxhall Motors*

The 1940s, by Alan D. Johnson

To explain what happened to mobile policing in the 1950s and '60s, we need to look back to events of the 1940s, for here was set a 'die' that would affect all that followed for nearly two decades. Whilst it is hard to conceive that what happened in 1939 would still be influencing the decision-makers 20-years on, that was certainly the case in 1959 when I found myself as a 'human resource' for the powers-that-be. It is more incredible to record that the decisions made in the late-1940s were still being implemented in the late-1960s, but that was the process of change, and in transport policy it was like kicking a dinosaur in the tail; it was a long time before the pain in its bum reached its head!

In 1939 most of the manufacturing companies were planning new car models for 1940, despite the Munich crisis of September 1938! During the war, the firms that had been used to building family cars suddenly found their production facilities turned over to important war work, for example the Vauxhall plant at Luton would turn out just over 100 cars in the next six years, although thousands of trucks and tanks were built.

Above: *How can anyone fail to be arrested, by the magnificence and absolute beauty of the RM series Riley This range of cars were in production from 1946 until 1955, although the 2.5-litre cars, in later RMF form lasted only until 1953 when they were replaced by the Pathfinder. West Sussex police, like many other forces, used such examples during the 1950s. This January 1948 example of the RMB (as the pale blue diamond badge portrays), is one of those fitted with the 2443cc four-cylinder engine that gave a top speed of 95mph.* Sussex Constabulary

Car purchase tax (introduced in October 1940) then combined with petrol rationing to reduce the demand for new cars. Personal or pleasure motoring was frowned upon, and with many people joining the forces cars were laid up for the duration. Further reduction in the petrol ration came in the Spring of 1942, when the limit was four or five gallons a month, but as the worst of the U-boat attacks decimated the Atlantic convoys, private motoring was banned completely in June of that year. Blackout restrictions and a 20mph night-time speed limit in built-up areas also had an effect at reducing the number of private cars on the road.

That is not to say that the police were idle during this time, quite the contrary, as the demands placed upon them and their resources became quite onerous. I recall a friend of my father who was made an Inspector with the Metropolitan Police in August 1939, just two weeks before World War II broke out. This man was a quarter-Argentinian and he had a mass of black curly hair, yet by 1945 his mane was as white as snow and he was still only 42-years of age. For most of the war he was on traffic duty and had special responsibility for co-ordinating emergency fire and ambulance movements in the East End, where he saw some of the most horrific aspects of the blitz.

Another friend, who I'll just call Bill was a sergeant with one of the railway police forces, and he had been given a big Ford V8 estate car, which had to double-up as an emergency ambulance as well as a police car. Following a bombing raid on a bonded warehouse in the docks area, he was called in to prevent looting, a task in which he was assisted by four special constables. The site they had to cover was around 40-acres, and although there were only two or three exits, it left just Bill and one special to patrol the site. Bottles of gin and rum (destined for the Royal Navy) were strewn all over the site, and many of these were still intact.

As the night wore on, the two patrolling officers found that the bottles were mysteriously vanishing from where they had fallen and it was obvious that someone was squirrelling them away. Imagine the surprise of the officers when they returned to the estate and found that one hoard had been hidden under a pile of blankets in the back.

Obviously someone had had the bright idea that the car would take the 'goods' past the police blockade, but they had obviously given little thought as to how they would be reclaimed later on. Bill, straight as the day was long handed over the bottles, but some months later, long after he handed the car over, a colleague said to him 'thanks for the gin, Bill' - a couple of bottles had been hidden under a seat and been missed in the gloom. Bill told me he must have driven those bottles around for a thousand miles and never knew they were there - "however", he winked "if they'd been bottles of rum it might have been a different story!"

Below: *This image of a 1939 Austin 16 with the Birmingham City Police force, takes one back to a time when the police were held in awe by children and the cars were exciting.*
West Midlands Police

Into The 1950s, by Alan D. Johnson & Robert Berry

In the introduction I mentioned the implementation of the new Motorway scheme as being a Conservative idea to rid Britain of its railways, as they viewed, the strength of the 'triple alliance' unions (coal, steel and railway workers) with considerable apprehension. Once the Suez crisis (and the associated petrol rationing) was over, the Minister of Transport Harold Watkins gave much more freedom to the road lobby.

However the plan they had outlined for the new Motorway networks as early as 1952-3 was not a new one, merely a re-vamp of a 1946 Labour idea called 'The Grand Plan', which envisaged a new network of trunk roads and 'Motor Roads'. Comparing a map of the 1946 plans with the network that was eventually constructed shows very few differences in the radial routes, for instance the 1946 plan even showed a Trans-Pennine crossing (M62). You have to begin somewhere though, and as unlikely as this may seem, it was decided this would be with an 8.25-mile by-pass of Preston, Lancashire.

Above: *Preston, the home of the first British motorway, was a crossroads in north-south, east-west traffic. It was also an important railway town for the same reason. Here we see the town's station in 1953, as it hosts the start of Blackpool FC's FA Cup 'Victory Parade' following their 4-3 victory over Bolton Wanderers at Wembley. The column is lead by Preston Borough Constabulary's Vauxhall Velox E Type.* Vauxhall Motors

At the time the A6 through Preston took the northbound traffic to Blackpool, the Lake District and Glasgow and at peak times huge tail-backs occurred as a consequence, so a by-pass was needed. In fact, the M6 would start out as a series of by-passes for major centres of population, Lancaster came next in 1960, then Stafford (1962), Penrith (1968) and Carlisle (1972), followed by longer stretches of motorway joining the by-passes together. The first of these non-by-pass sections was the section between Hanchurch and Barthomley (J15-16) in 1962, and the last was the stretch between Gravelly Hill and Great Barr in Birmingham (J6-7) that opened ten-years later.

The engineer for the project, James (later Sir James) Drake took the Preston By-pass through to completion on 31st October 1958, despite atrocious weather problems during 1956 and difficulties with the concrete on the Samlesbury Bridge. In view of the significance of the event, the ceremony was performed by the Prime Minister, Harold Macmillan on 5th December 1958, and a granite plinth marking the occasion was erected at the Samlesbury interchange.

A few months later, at 3pm in the afternoon of Monday 24th March 1959 to be precise, the work on The London - Birmingham Motorway (M1) was commenced, when the first sod was cut in a field beside the hamlet of Slip End, near Luton, to say the first sod was cut is not strictly true as the then Minister of Transport, the Rt, Hon. Harold Watkinson, merely pressed a button which sounded a klaxon summoning into action (throughout 53-miles of countryside) an enormous concentration of mechanical power. So, at a time when Britain's principle trunk roads filed through towns causing bottle-necks and very long delays, the new motorway age with its wide carriageways and low elevations was promoted as the way to rid congestion on the roads and the (cynic in me says) provide a reason to get rid of the railways!

By way of a contrast with the austere post-war period of the 1940s, the mood of the 1950s was, one of optimism, and this proved to be a period of greater prosperity throughout the country. British car producers appeared to be striving to meet the public demand for new cars as motoring finally broke free from the post-war shortages. Petrol Rationing had ended in 1950, but was then re-introduced with the Suez Crisis in 1956-7, but generally the atmosphere for the motorist had lightened considerably as the new motorways opened. The combined results of long waiting lists for new cars, plus the attraction of fuel now being in plentiful supply, caused the prices of second-hand cars to become almost as competitive as new car prices when they were available. Oddly, for a while, the second-hand market was often the route some police forces chose for the cars that were at first in production in the post- war period.

Below: *As the Lancashire County Constabulary was at the forefront of motorway policing, we have given considerable attention to this force's requirements in this book. This 1956 view shows seven fine Vauxhall Velox patrol cars, but other vehicles in the fleet included Hillman, Humber and Austin. Vauxhall Motors*

Top Left: *Upholding the law and preventing crime was perhaps the prime functions of the police, but just as important is the service that they extend to the welfare and safety of the community. This officer from the Lancashire County Constabulary leaves the comfort of his Vauxhall Velox to check nobody is skating on a frozen pond that had been declared unsafe after a child had tragically died there previously. A chalked warning on the fence poignantly reads "Keep off the ice -remember what happened last time."* Vauxhall Motors

Middle Left: *Austin produced 316,484 examples of their A40 Dorset and Devon models between 1947 and 1952. Styled very much on the smaller car's design were the 2.2-litre A70 Hampshire models that were introduced in 1948. This West Riding of Yorkshire County Constabulary car is one of the 35,261 A70 vehicles built.* West Yorkshire Police

Bottom Left: *A vehicle that I was much more associated with buying for the red and green liveries of the General Post Office fleets of the 1950s. This is a utilicon version of the Morris model J van, serving with the Lothian Police force. The Morris is fitted with a radio telephone and was thought to be equipped to deal with 'any situation that may arise'.* Lothain and Borders Police

By the early-1950s, many of the country's police forces found that a significant increase was still needed in their motor patrols. Due to a shortage of new cars, some forces tended to buy second-hand vehicles in the early post-war years, as the motor industry was exhorted to 'Export or Die'. However, with the improving situation in the motor industry, more new cars were becoming available for the home market, including police forces.

For example, Austin were producing their 'County' range, among the early ones were the four-door Devon and the two-door Dorset models. Commercial versions of the Devon were also produced and these also proved popular with many forces, particularly as radio cars. A larger model, styled on the Devon was the 2199cc Hampshire. These were produced from 1948 to 1950 with a total of 35,261 being built during this time, whilst the smaller 1200cc Devon and Dorset variants reached production figures of 316,484 between 1947 and 1952

The City of Birmingham took delivery of no less than 15 Hampshire cars, which had inherited the 2.2-litre engine from the Austin 16 models; many of which had also served as police cars, Birmingham included. These models performed well enough, but it was a rather bulbous car that had primarily been designed for the export market in line with the demand from government. These cars, although larger than the Devon, do not appear to have had much extra interior space for the occupants, They were also fitted with a column gear-change, which was rather difficult in operation. Added to this, they were fitted with hydro-mechanical brakes that lacked feel, so they were not ideal for fulfiling the role of a rapid police car.

The number of private cars in major towns had reached the point of almost epidemic proportions during the mid-1950s, with London and several principle towns and cities often in the grip of a deadlock. This would often bring about complete chaos, and also resulted in angry or frustrated drivers making the situation worse. Many police forces would operate 'Courtesy Patrols', which were designed to lessen the stretched resources of the force and to merely caution the motorist for minor infringements of the law.

At this time, proceedings were only taken for extreme cases of motoring offences, such as dangerous driving or excessive speeding etc. The prevention of accidents was the key role of these patrols, yet there was the ever-increasing problem of congestion in the crowded streets and obstructions were exacerbating the problem too. The police had the powers to enforce parking restrictions and could even have vehicles causing unnecessary obstruction towed to the police station vehicle compound at the owner's expense.

The 1950s saw much more reliance on technical development taking place throughout the police force. Among the advances introduced during this period was the use of radar to record vehicle speeds, whilst experiments were taking place with such devices as on-board cameras to record incidents of vehicles being driven in a dangerous manner. Then, as now, such devices were not at all popular with the general motoring public. However, the Home Office's concern (and principle consideration) was to save the lives of those drivers who were all-to-often ill-prepared for the road. As an example we might state that even the problem of tyre wear was of little concern to some drivers. In talks with the Ministry of Transport, it was decided that some form of testing would be needed to ensure that all vehicles would be roadworthy and that enforcing any new regulations would be the responsibility of the police. As a result of this, in 1960 the Minister of Transport Mr Ernest Marples, decided that all vehicles over ten-years-old should have their brakes, lights and steering checked every year. This ten year period was ultimately reduced to three-years.

Top Right: *Herbert Austin would have been proud of this line up of three Austin A70 Hereford cars that served with the Devon & Cornwall Constabulary.* Devon & Cornwall Police Museum

Middle Right: *From the earliest times of the motorisation of the British police forces, vehicle purchasing policy was entirely devoted to British-built vehicles. This policy remained unchanged until the 1960s. Among the more popular choices were Vauxhall. Ford, Morris, and as we see by this illustration Austin. This 1955 example was operated by the City Of Bradford Police.* West Yorkshire Constabulary

Bottom Right: *Part of the fleet of the Devon & Cornwall police force during the 1950s shows a brace of the A95 Westminsters, followed by an A70 Hereford with an early Bedford CA at the rear.* Devon & Cornwall Police Museum

Above: *From the remarkable amount of paraphernalia on display here, one would assume that Lancashire Constabulary's 1958 Ford Zephyr Farnham estate car has an interior akin to Doctor Who's 'TARDIS'. This patrol car had a 2553cc six-cylinder engine and a three-speed gearbox, and was a design approved by Alan Johnson for a role in motorway policing.* Lancashire Constabulary

The 1950s marked the period when police vehicles were not only viewed as a means of mobility, but as a mobile office from which officers were expected to deal with any type of situation that might arise during the course of their day. Thus not only was the latest technology of paramount interest, but the actual vehicles themselves were also, expected to be ultra-reliable. As the above view shows, the new, fast patrol cars had to be capable of carrying an enormous amount of equipment and warning devices to help the motorist.

Some forces, like the Lancashire Constabulary, very quickly motorised as the road network improved in their area, and the advent of the Preston By-pass in 1958 put this county first. Lancashire was one of the largest forces in the country, and by the end of the decade, it had 280 cars of various makes with which to patrol its area. During the 1950s they used a wide variety of vehicles from the early Ford Pilots and the E Series Vauxhall Velox, to the more luxurious and graceful Jaguars of the time. Perhaps their most well-known were the Ford Zephyr models or the spritely MG sports cars .

Many police forces used small light sports cars on traffic control, but such was the limited amount of luggage space in these cars that the equipment was carried at the sacrifice of the spare wheel; when one was needed they simply phoned in for it. The fast patrol cars like the various MG models were very popular with their crews, but were still readily justified by their ease of manoeuvrability.

Sports models had often been bought prior to World War II, but they understandably retained their popularity, as they had the agility to negotiate slow moving traffic and were less cumbersome than more traditional machines and more economical in operation too. The versatility of these small cars also weighed heavily against using large, powerful American sedans that were initially given consideration for the 'Motor Way Patrol', a name euphemistically derived from the American 'Highway Patrol'.

The MG fast patrol cars approved for 'motorway work' in the north west of England were MG-A models, but these were not the first of the breed of sportscars to be operated by Lancashire police. In fact the MG-As had actually superseded MG-TF models, which in turn had replaced earlier TD examples. When new, seven of the MG-As were delivered in black and a further ten in white. These sports cars may seem rather removed from the normal idea of what a police car should look like, but Lancashire were not alone in the idea that there was a need for this type of vehicle. Warwickshire for instance had purchased six MG TC models back in 1946, whilst Oxford had also bought similar models. In London, the Daimler SP 25 sportscar was used extensively by the Metropolitan Police and other forces soon followed suit. The following decades would see the Triumph TR4A and Spitfire entering into several force fleets, whilst others chose the MG-C and the Sunbeam Tiger. The main drawback with light sportscars for police patrol work was their very limited carrying capacity in terms of both men and equipment. With a couple of burly police officers in the cockpit they would feel more than a little cramped, and the boot space was minuscule.

In truth the vast cross-section of the British police cars were chosen from the 'approved' list by senior officers to satisfy a certain role. Costs and delivery schedules also entered into this process, but they all had to fulfil one particular criterion; they had to be British! However such was the diversity of the British motor industry at that time, their was plenty of models to chose from.

Top Right: *Wolseley cars were very popular with the police right to the end of production of this marque, particularly so with the City of London and the Metropolitan forces. This 1955 example of a Series II Wolseley 6/90 model served with the Hertfordshire Constabulary.* Courtesy Nigel Scott

Middle Right: *During 1956, Ford introduced their MkII versions of the Zodiac, Zephyr and Consul range. Whilst the Zephyr achieved universal appeal with a large number of police forces, the four-cylinder Consul models were far less common. One example of the Consul that served with the police is PKY 334, which was with the City of Bradford.* West Yorkshire Constabulary

Bottom Right: *Hertfordshire Constabulary had a fondness for the products of Austin. This is an example of one of the A99 Westminster models that were produced during the late-1950s.* Courtesy Nigel Scott

Above: *These Vauxhall police cars were far removed from the more common vehicles chosen in the earlier part of the 1950s. On the left we see a brace of the luxurious six-cylinder Velox PAS models, on the right a Victor F-Type. Both models were introduced during 1957 to replace the four- and six-cylinder E series Vauxhall Wyvern and Velox cars that shared the same bodyshell.* Vauxhall Motors

Although Wolseley were typical of the police cars used during the 1940s and '50s, a very wide variety of vehicles were chosen. Gone were the days when cars were simply chosen for the transportation of the high ranking officials, as motorised policing took on an ever-more crucial role. Obviously conceding to these greater demands, the vehicles had, by necessity, to be furnished with a higher degree of equipment to enable them to deal with any situation that might occur in their working days.

Trials were undertaken by the Acquisition, Certification and Inspection Section during the late-1950s in an effort to find more suitable vehicles for the equipment that would have to be carried, especially on motorway work. Among the vehicles that were tried were the Humber Super Snipe, Standard Vanguard and Ford Zephyr estate cars.

All these cars were powered by an engine in the 2- to 2.6-litre size range, and they were often referred to as Incident Cars and would speed to the scene of a traffic accident or serious crime. The Metropolitan Police were well pleased with their Humber Snipe estate cars, while the Lancashire Constabulary made extensive use of the Ford Zephyr Mk II, versions of which had been converted to estate cars by the coachbuilders E.D. Abbott of Farnham. When the new MkIII Zephyr arrived on the scene in 1962, these were also chosen in both saloon and estate car form.

Above: *The products of Rover became very popular with a number of police forces after the introduction of the P6 models in 1964. Prior to this, although Police Commissioners had chosen the P5 model, few of Rover's other models entered police service. One exception however was the P4 model, which was built for over a decade. Among the police forces who chose this model were Cheshire who painted their cars in a deep green colour and Newport; the example illustrated here is a 1960 Rover 100 model.* R.W. Berry Collection

Right: *Most of the various Wolseley models were well used by the police, as many old black and white movie films clearly portray. In particular the larger series, such as the 6/90 and 6/110 cars were popular, but other models too were used, including the compact Wolseley 8 shown here.* Trans-Pennine Archive

Above and Left: *From a lofty vantage point above the M1, the crew of a Vauxhall Velox PB model keep an eye on the motorway traffic. These models started production life in 1962 with the 2.6-litre engine that was carried over from the late PA range. Halfway through their model life however, the Velox and more luxurious Cresta were both equipped with a new 3.3-litre 115bhp engine. When the Vauxhall Cresta and Velox PB models were replaced by new designs in 1965, it was also decided to discontinue the use of Velox as a model name. Two models of the new PC range of cars were available from the outset however, both powered by the 3.3-litre engine from the later PB models. The names were now Cresta and Cresta Deluxe. Instantly recognised from the front of the car, you can tell that this is the more basic model by its single headlights. This PC Cresta model is a Vauxhall demonstrartor on trial with the Bedfordshire Constabulary.* Vauxhall Motors

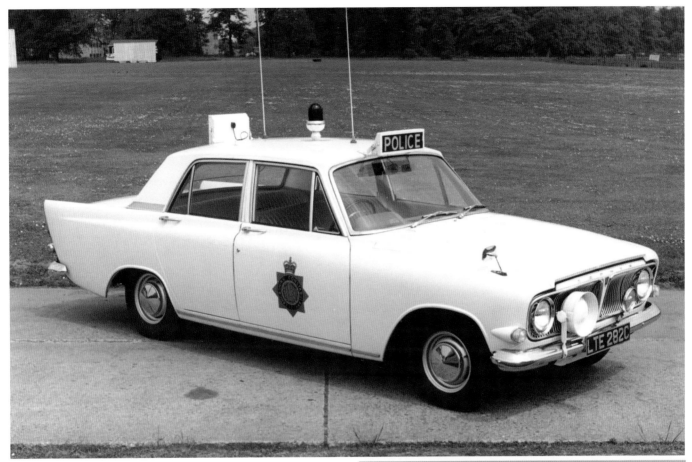

Above: *The attractive, practical and reliable MkIII version of the Ford Zephyr 6 (in service with Lancashire Constabulary) was the latest fashion for motorway patrol cars during the 1960s. Perhaps their greatest claim to fame was their starring role in the BBC television series* Z Cars, *which was about a modern police force set in the fictional Lancashire area called Newtown.*
Lancashire Constabulary

Right: *Rather surprisingly, a number of police forces chose to use various sportscars for their motorway patrols, whilst some other forces used them as area cars. Although they were limited in their ability of load area, they made up for this in their operational use. This view of an MG-B shows it is very little different from the civilian cars of the day, but note the radio, the discrete police signs and the blue lamps on the off-side wings.*
Lancashire Constabulary

Above and Left: *During the 1960s, police forces introduced 'Unit Policing', which was at a time when many police forces were suffering an acute man-power shortage. Police officers that usually walked their beat or the more rural based ones on bicycles, were now motorised with economical small saloon cars. These cars were usually painted in a very distinctive livery of a turquoise blue with white doors and a broad white band across the roof, thus known as 'Panda Cars'. Although police forces chose different types of the many popular two-door saloon cars that were on the market at that time to serve as 'Panda Cars'. Some models such as the Ford Anglia, Morris Minor and Vauxhall Viva became almost synonymous with the role. The Ford Anglia model proved so popular as 'Panda Cars', that Ford actually had them painted and fully finished to police standards on their own production lines at Halewood.*
Ford Motor Company (upper) and
Lancashire Constabulary (lower)

THE 1960s by Robert Berry

As the 'Fabulous Fifties' gave way to the 'Swinging Sixties', a contrast in social change (of the kind that had rarely been seen before) began to take place in a sudden and somewhat turbulent manner. Architecture, fashion, industry and music all played their part in forming this new decade, but it was clearly a time when youth discovered it had an identity, as people began demanding greater levels of personal freedom.

This was a time that saw many changes both within the police forces and the public perception of them, especially as motorisation led to what some people called the isolation of the police and the public. In previous decades, British society had been comforted by the typical bobby on the street, who's popular image was that of a rather burly, robust character who stood no nonsense, one knew that within that formidable and trustworthy frame beat a heart of gold.

Above: *Rather unusually, Stockport police chose various examples of Vauxhall Motors PA Velox models. This early-1960s view shows from left to right, PDB 514 a 2.2-litre PAS model, then four of the 2.6-litre PASX models, two of the PASY types, and finally NDB 752, which is a second PAS.* Vauxhall Motors

However this stalwart of the British way of life was suddenly no more as he was replaced by the new method of community policing , whereby a police officer was motorised with a unit beat car or 'Panda'. This was inevitably seen by the majority of the public as a alienation of them by the police force. Yet the reasoning of this method was fundamentally sound, as five such vehicles could effectively cover the same beats as eleven officers could do on foot. Yet because of this move, the important personal relationship between the officers of the law and the law-abiding citizens suddenly and sadly became quite impersonal.

Top Left: *During 1959, dated models from the BMC stable were gradually replaced with new models that were designed by Farina for the 1960s. The third exercise was the Austin A99 Westminster, which was introduced to replace the five-year-old Austin A95/105 models. These A99 models, like this 1959 example serving with the West Riding of Yorkshire Constabulary, were powered by a 2.9-litre six-cylinder engine.* West Yorkshire Constabulary

Middle and Bottom Left: *Although Vauxhall have produced many types of police car, the PA models of the 1950-60 period were not that plentiful in police service. The PADX/PASX were introduced during 1960 and the original 2.2-litre engine was replaced by one of 2.6-litre capacity. This example is still black and carries a bell, but note the illuminated sign carried on the front of the appropriately registered BBM 999. The back view of the PASX Velox clearly illustrates the rear lights, which were unique to this model. The two previous series had full height oval units with the flashing indicators set in the end of the flights where this chrome 'V' is set.* both Vauxhall Motors

In addition to the 'isolation' of the police, the liveries employed on their vehicles were about to change too, and not for much longer would we see the traditional big black British police cars, with the familiar bell. The larger 'Incident' or 'Area' cars would be gradually superseded by white vehicles with sirens, again though this was all said to be done in the interests of modernisation, efficiency and safety. Even more daring colour schemes would come with the 'beat' vehicles, which would become universally known as Pandas. To many this was an American idea, and whilst the entertainment medium of television still had the British favourites such as *Gideon's Way* starring John Gregson or Jack Warner in *Dixon of Dock Green*, the 1960s saw many arrivals of the American police heroes. These included such as Efram Zimbalist Jnr. in *77 Sunset Strip* and its clone, *Hawaiian Eye*, with Grant Williams and Troy Donaghue.

During the 1960s, the law of the land was often criticised too, for with the abolishment of capital punishment, violent crime was perceived to be on the increase. Yet the hands of the police were tied as they tried to serve two masters, the general public and the law courts. Even after all this time most readers will readily recall such serious crimes as the 'Great Train Robbery' or the 'Moors Murders'. Some crimes seemed to merit different levels of prosecution, than the more serious ones of homicide; but this book is not intending to review the merits of the law, merely reflecting on the changes witnessed during this period.

The amalgamation of various police forces continued through the 1960s, as some of the smaller police forces were combined into larger forces and County Constabularies. Some of these were justifiably proud of their independence and history being established in the very infancy of the police services, and it took some compulsion from the Home Office to achieve this.

Above: *If I think back to when I was a boy in Yorkshire, I can clearly remember the local police having similar vehicles to these, however this pair of Ford Zephyrs operated on the other side of the Pennines.* Greater Manchester Police Museum

With the inauguration of the new motorway system, it was thought that a new national force might be created as a division of the British Transport Police. However, a decision was then taken by the Home Office and Ministry of Transport to pay local police forces to provide patrols for sections of motorway in their respective areas. The officers who were to maintain these patrols were then specially selected and given advanced driver training.

Between the time when the motorway was opened in 1958 and 1965, there was no speed limit on the motorway plus (as mentioned earlier in our text) there was an obvious need to remove potential dangers from the area such as stray animals and dangerous vehicles. This period was also a time before the MoT Test was introduced. Consequently there were a lot of vehicles using the motorway when they were neither suitable or capable of sustaining long or fast cruising speeds; as a result abandoned or broken-down vehicles were common. The motorways had been designed and built with an eight-foot wide hard shoulder, for use in emergencies or by stranded vehicles or those involved in a collision, as they would need the aid of the police and other breakdown or emergency services.

As the motorway network grew, it was decided that specific vehicles would be purchased for this role. A task with which Alan D. Johnson was long involved, he wrote: "As long as they were British, cars were simply chosen for their high cruising speed and ease of manoeuvrability. After 1965, they had to be capable of at least 90mph, in order to catch motorists exceeding the new 70mph speed limits. Ford, Vauxhall and Rover all looked at engine modifications that could squeeze an extra five-miles-per-hour out of what would often be a heavily loaded car."

The speed limit was introduced in an effort to reduce the amount of traffic accidents that were becoming far too common on the motorways, at a time when little consideration was given to the capability of the drivers or of the vehicles being driven; not to mention driver fatigue or drink-driving.

Top Left: *Although less common as a motorway patrol car, one or two police forces chose the Humber Super Snipe for this role. This included Hertfordshire who acquired this estate version in 1964.*

Middle Left: *Archetypical among the marques that were associated with police forces during the 1960s was Jaguar. Among the fleet of Dumfries and Galloway Constabulary was this unmarked 1959 Jaguar Mk II car painted in an unusual pale blue colour.* Dumfries & Galloway Constabulary

Bottom Left: *Typifying Lancashire's motorway patrol cars during the late-1950s and early-'60s are these two vehicles. On the right is one of the nimble MG-As, while the left-hand car is one of the Ford Zephyr MkII estate cars by Abbott of Farnham.* Greater Manchester Police Museum

Although police cars were traditionally painted either black or dark blue, the Chief Constable of the Lancashire Constabulary (Colonel Eric St-Johnston) introduced white as a colour scheme for motorway patrol cars when the Preston By-pass opened. Although this did not achieve Home office approval at first, it was soon to become the normal practice for motorway patrol cars. This gave them a highly visible profile, which was considered as both a deterrent and a safety aspect for a stationary vehicle on the motorway. Later the uniform for this branch of police work would incorporate white tops to the officers' hats. Col. St-Johnston, who had formerly been the Chief Constable with the Durham force also introduced radar speed traps into the Lancashire area.

With the pale colours becoming ever more popular as a choice of paint on private motor vehicles, white police cars became far less conspicuous. In the effort to counteract this problem and add further to the safety of the officers who patrolled the expanding motorway network in all kinds of weather (night and day), Col. St-Johnston then introduced the 'Day-Glo Orange' and white colour schemes to the motorway patrol cars of Lancashire that were used on the M6. Again this did not initially meet with official approval, but was later widely adopted by many other forces. One of the early converts was the Staffordshire Constabulary (who also patrolled the M6), as they painted their MkII Jaguar saloon cars this way. These were principally white, but they had this extremely vibrant and eye-catching vivid orange on panels such as the boot lid.

While we are on the subject of colour schemes on police vehicles, the 1960s was the period that 'Unit Policing' and 'Panda Cars' were introduced. Alan Johnson writes: "A decision was made to take economical cars like the Ford Anglia or BMC Mini, and give a distinctive white band on both the front doors and the roof. As black was the first basic body colour used, they looked like Panda bears. For this reason we came up with the anacronym, 'Patrol and neighbourhood deployment area cars', although when Ford offered a substantial discount on their Anglia from the production line, we could only get them in pale blue and white."

The first Panda patrols were carried out in Lancashire (a pioneering force in many ways), although this was due to the fact that the cars were on loan from the Ford plant at Halewood where the Anglia was made. The Pandas did not suit everyone though, for instance having a policeman on the beat offered a sense of security to the elderly, for this had been a way of life to these people. Even members of the police force themselves conceded later that, with the introduction of the unit beat patrol, something was lost in the relationships between the police and the public.

Unit policing was however seen as a way of making the police far more versatile and more readily able to answer an emergency call. Arguably it began in the Kirkby area of Liverpool in 1965 using five Anglia cars from Ford at Halewood, but the cars had actually been initially tested in the Preston area during 1964. Economical to purchase and operate, they were also reliable and easy to manoeuvre, so they were considered ideal for testing in the newly designed role. From these experiments, came the common Panda cars that soon became familiar on the streets of Britain. When Ford offered a production line option of the Anglia Panda, they were taken up by a large number of forces.

Above: *The MkIII Ford Zephyr Six estate like this West Yorkshire example, that entered the fleet during 1966 was an ideal motorway patrol car. Particularly in estate car format with its adequate load area. Following the established principles of Lancashire for high-visibility for their motorway patrol cars, this white Zephyr was finished with reflective red and dark blue stripes.*
West Yorkshire Constabulary

Even so, other manufacturers had their share of the emerging market, for instance BMC supplied the Morris Minor saloon (plus the Traveller), they also offered the ubiquitous Mini; even the rather spartan Mini Moke served in places like Wales and Dartmoor. Vauxhall had the HA Viva saloon, whilst the Rootes Group offered both the Hillman Minx and the Hillman Imp. Meanwhile other police forces tried examples of BMC Morris and Austin 1100/1300 models as unit beat cars. In addition to the increasing use of the Panda car, the van versions of many of the above models soon acheived popularity for mobile police dog patrols as well; especially at a time when dogs were starting to play an increasingly significant role in the modern policing methods of the time.

Top Left: *Just looking at this photograph of a Morris Minor taken at the West Riding of Yorkshire headquarters in Wakefield, one can immediately hear the van's distinctive engine sound. This was just one of many police forces that chose these reliable vans, to serve their dog patrol sections.* West Yorkshire Constabulary

Middle Left: *Manchester Longsight Police Station was the home of this Morris LD prison van. These vehicles were based on the 30 -cwt commercial and were a natural choice for the role of prison van, as the interior space in these conventional vans was ideal.* Greater Manchester Police

Bottom Left: *Another example of a special commercial vehicle in police use is being driven by Constable Tom Whalley of the Southend-on-Sea County Borough Constabulary. This is an Austin A152 Omnivan Emergency and Rescue patrol van, complete with a Beaufort dinghy, which was used to patrol the sea-fronts during the summer months.* Essex Police courtesy Nigel Scott

The testing of Panda cars in 1965 had impressive results. In Kirkby, reported crime dropped by a third and detection rates went up by 91%. Accrington was the first town in the country to get the Panda cars after the decision had been made, but by 1967 they were on duty county-wide in Lancashire. Police morale soared and one report at the time noted: "They now feel able to deal more effectively with any situation which may arise, knowing that any calls for assistance will bring immediate help. This has considerably reduced the number of assaults on police officers, which was part of the enjoyment of gangs of hooligans whose courage evaporates when faced by more than one policeman."

Interestingly, despite the general acknowledgement about Kirkby being the first town to use Pandas, the *Kirkby Times* web-site actually attributes the first Panda cars to the Midlands, where BMC held trials with the Birmingham and Worcestershire. Speaking of the introduction of the Panda cars, the newspaper says: "That was in the days when Kirkby and other towns in Liverpool and elsewhere had coppers who actually stayed around long enough to know who was who, before the Police Force became so unpopular that it needed to drive around certain areas at high speed, dropping the local beat for a few radio linked cars. An experiment which began in Birmingham in the 1960s led to a dramatic change in Police working practices. The Panda Car alienated the Police from the Public. The cops left on the beat were encountering a more and more hostile and mistrustful Public. People no longer volunteered information and so paid informants took off. In the UK this meant that informants received cash payments for informing on various crimes."

Alan Johnson could not recall who was first with the Panda cars, but says that: "Both Ford and the BMC were submitting cars for evaluation, primarily the Anglia and the Minor 1000 respectively; but I think these may have been simultaneously with one another."

One of the important roles that police vehicles still had to perform was that of the traditional prison van, for as will be recalled such vehicles had been among the earliest forms of motorised police transport. The earliest examples had of course succeeded the original horse-drawn vehicles, but because of their reasonably limited and unpopular use, they tended to be rather overlooked. Such vehicles as these were more often than not purchases of the conventional vans that were in production at the time, but were then improvised for their role by the fitting of security features. Perhaps among the most common were the BMC LD models that were to be seen serving in many forces during the 1950s and '60s.

Other similar types of vehicle were also chosen for specific roles, such as the mini-buses used to transfer police officers for crowd control at events like public displays or football matches. Even examples of various buses and coaches were purchased by certain constabularies for this role, notably the economical Bedford OB during the 1940s and '50s and the Bedford SB in the 1960s.

The Morris J served in some rural fleets as a general purpose utility vehicle, whilst other forces used the very popular Bedford CA in either van or mini-bus form. Then there were vehicles like the Austin J2 Dormobile, one complete with roof-mounted inflated raft, which was owned by the Southend-on-Sea Constabulary as an Emergency & Rescue Patrol van that patrolled the sea-front during the summer months. By the mid- to late-1960s, many police forces were entrusting these roles to the popular Ford Transit vans. These became commonplace in perhaps the majority of police forces through-out the British Isles from the 1960s onwards, and they are covered in a **Nostalgia Road** book on the history of this model.

Top Right: *Police forces often promoted public relation exercises and displays throughout the country. Here in 1959 we see one such event, where 18 new MG-As of the Lancashire Constabulary are about to perform a series of exercises set to music.* Courtesy Andrew J. Fowlie

Middle Right: *This 2.5-litre Daimler SP250 seen at Hendon is possibly the Metropolitan Police force's 549 CLU, although it may be one of the other 1961 models from the same batch. The style of these glass-fibre bodied roadsters was not to everyone's taste, but they had a very powerful engine, of a type that was also fitted into the Daimler 2.5-litre V8. saloon, the model Jaguar introduced soon after their take-over of the long established Daimler company.* Metropolitan Police

Bottom Right: *Confident in the knowledge that his steed is more than a match for the interesting collection of vehicles in the background (and with an American Ford 4.2-litre engine under the bonnet) anything else on the city streets for that matter. The smile on the face of the City of Leeds police officer is almost as wide as that on this 1966 Series I Sunbeam Tiger.* West Yorkshire Constabulary

THE CARS, by Robert W. Berry

After the formation of the Metropolitan Police Act in 1829, then the Municipal Corporation Act of 1835 required all municipal boroughs and corporations to set up their own Borough Police Services. Back then the principle form of transport for all police officers (excluding the local Chief Constable and some senior officers) was on foot. As mentioned earlier in our text, the majority of the watch committees who were at first responsible for the police forces in their infancy. decreed that the aforesaid Chief Constables would be allowed and provided with a horse and carriage. This obviously was to allow them to visit the police stations that they were responsible for. It also afforded them the respect that their position demanded and set them apart from the conventional police officer's. Later other forms of horse-drawn police vehicles, and the use of bicycles became widespread, but motoring law would soon feature prominent in police work around the country.

Above: *Vauxhall Motors were a favourite choice of many police forces from the very start of their motorisation. One of the more popular models of the 1950s were the E series Velox. These cars were powered by a powerful 2.2-litre engine, and also benefited from a commodious boot and comfortable interior. This example is another one to serve with Lancashire Constabulary.*
Vauxhall Motors

One of the first motor laws came in 1896 with the Locomotives on the Highway Act. This new legislation removed many restrictions on motoring and made vehicles weighing less than three-tons exempt from the earlier stringent requirements that had deterred motoring, which were part of the Locomotive Act 1865 and imposed a speed limit of 2mph in built-up areas, and 4mph in the countryside. This Act had not only required a pedestrian carrying a red flag in front of the vehicle at a distance of 60 yards, but also insisted that the vehicle had to have three drivers aboard it.

In 1896, with the changes under the new Act, the speed limit was raised to 14mph. However under the new Act, vehicle lights were then required, along with some form of audible warning. In addition, every heavy locomotive had to be registered by local county or county borough council in the area where it was based. Yet, not everyone liked the idea of the automobile, especially in country towns, where they were accused of 'startling horses', 'causing an uproar', 'disturbing the peace' and other such infamous deeds. Rural police forces and magistrates, influenced by the landowners, often declared all out war on motorists, and speed traps were literally as the name implies. Indeed, the first speeding ticket was issued on 28th January 1896, when Walter Arnold was fined one shilling (5p) for travelling at 8mph in a 2mph area.

Of course, there was a necessity for the motor vehicle to be 'regulated', especially after Britain's first motoring fatality occurred at Crystal Palace, London on 17th August that year, when a Mrs Bridget Driscoll of Old Town, Croydon, was run over. By 1897 it seemed that the motorist was 'fair game' for the police courts, and there was no organisation to protect them, until the proposed formation of an Automobile Club in 1897.

More regulations followed in the Motor Car Act 1903, which required that all vehicles had to be registered, and to display registration marks in a prominent position. The fee was twenty shillings (£1). The first registration marks consisted of one letter and one number, the first (A1) was issued by London County Council. Other cities and towns were also allocated specific letter codes and when these were exhausted two letter codes were issued. Driving licences were also introduced, but they were easily obtained by paying a fee of five shillings (25p) across the counter at a Post Office. At this time they were used merely for identification purposes, and were becoming more widely needed due to the 'large numbers of drivers giving false names and addresses to the county police' following an 'arrest' for motoring offences. The speed limit was however raised to 20mph, but if you went over this there were even heavier fines for speeding.

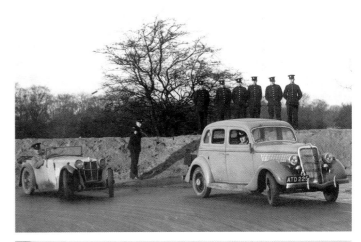

Top Right: *Photographed at one of the specially established police driving schools. Police Trainee drivers under instruction, stand at a clear and safe vantage point as a little MG (perhaps a 1931-2 Magna), pursues a 1935 Ford V8 model 48 Fordor saloon.* Lancashire Constabulary

Middle and Bottom Right: *With the coming of the motorisation, special police driver training schools were set up throughout the country. This was to achieve the highest standard of driving and also acquire the relevant skills and experience of handling cars in any given situation. The vehicles that were used at these schools were usually second-hand examples or police cars that had reached the end of their service life. In these two photographs a Ford Zephyr is put through its paces by the Liverpool City/police driving school. Courtesy Tony Roache*

Top Left: *In 1958 serious consideration was given to using a big American saloon for the 'MotorWay Police', which was initially thought might become a national force under the British Transport Police. The car considered for this work, on account of its size, power and modest price, was the Oldsmobile Dynamic 88 (1958 - 1966), which was usually powered by a lower horsepower Rocket V8 engine than its Super 88 and 98 counterparts.* A. D. Johnson

Middle Left: *Another type that was considered for fast patrol work in 1958 was the Armstrong Siddeley 234/236 Sapphire. These were often referred to as the 'Baby Sapphires', but being powered by a 2.3-litre engine and being only an inch shorter than a MkII Jaguar they were certainly not diminutive.* A. D. Johnson

Bottom Left: *Although many different cars were tried for the role of fast motorway patrol cars. The universal favourites were from Ford, Vauxhall and Jaguar, as seen with this Jaguar MkII model. These were powered by a choice of 2.4, 3.4 or 3.8 litre engines. This example is viewed at Manchester Longsight Police station.* Greater Manchester Police courtesy Nigel Scott

Many police forces were very slow to achieve any degree of motorisation; take Southampton for example. Although requests were put forward to the watch committee, for the replacement of their horse-drawn 'Black Maria' by a motorised vehicle, the request was shelved until after World War I, when a Piece Arrow police van finally embarked upon a degree of motorisation. Later in the decade during 1925, an AJS motorcycle combination was purchased by the force. Three police officers were especially chosen to operate this machine on a shift principle. This experiment proved to be sufficiently successful that three years later, three more similar types of machines followed.

This was not an uncommon story, and the motorbike or combination were the principle method by which the British police forces became motorised in the 1920s and '30s. Even so, the basic method of policing was still by foot patrols and would remain so until the 1960s, especially in the major cities and large towns. Communications between police officers and their fellow beat colleagues or their 'stations', was primarily done by whistle blasts, which would be repeated to enable assistance to be summoned. Then, at Albany (New York) in 1877, the first five police telephones were installed to connect the Mayor's Office with five police districts in the city. Washington, Chicago and Boston followed, and by 1885 it was considered a resounding success.

Telegraphy systems had been employed in British policing since the mid-1870s, but Glasgow was one of the first to make a public service by using 82 'Alarm Boxes' to call out the city's fire service (which was operated by the police). The same city can claim responsibility for the first Police Alarm Box, which was produced to a patent by Charles Eggar, a local fireman and made from cast-iron by McFarlen & Co. of the Saracen Foundry, Glasgow.

Glasgow remained pre-eminent in police communications, and most other cities followed their lead, including London. By 1931 Glasgow's new Chief Constable, Percy (later Sir Percy) Sillitoe, announced he wanted to improve the efficiency of police mobility. He thus addressed a meeting of senior officers from the city, and wrote a paper to all other Chief Constables, stating: "The police force was far too inefficient. The ratio of crimes committed to crimes detected was too low and too many police officers were acting like little more than public night watchmen."

Re-organisations suggested by Sillitoe envisaged savings of £28,000 per annum, and he decided to spend this money on technology, including new cars and a more modern system. The boxes he proposed would be developed from the ones designed by Sir George McKenzie Trench for the Metropolitan Police in 1929, but would effectively be made into miniature police stations. The history of the police 'phone box is fascinating, and we ought to make mention of the developments in Newcastle and Sheffield, but as the primary consideration of this book is police cars, we must swiftly pass over these. Save to say that one full-sized replica that appeared in an early episode of the BBC's *Z Cars* series, went on to achieve screen immortality as the TARDIS of *Doctor Who* fame.

Sillitoe was also influenced by the development of two-way radio cars, which had begun in the United States in 1921 when mobile radios began operating at 2MHz, just above the present AM radio broadcast band. The first radio systems were one-way, sometimes using Morse Code, with police getting out of their cars and then calling their station house on a wired telephone after being paged. Their use began in Britain with Home Office experiments starting in 1927, the same year as two-way trans-Atlantic radio was introduced. Sillitoe had seriously considered the wider use of radio when he was the Chief Constable of Sheffield, but it was only when he moved to Glasgow, that he was able to fully experiment between radio-controlled cars and a HQ radio station, and in turn link these with his 'beat boxes'. Amongst Sillitoe's other innovations was the distinctive black and white diced cap bands, which became known as the 'Sillitoe Tartan'.

Top Right: *Here we see a WPC serving with Kent Constabulary and one of their handsome 1962 Sunbeam Rapier IIIA saloon cars. These were really high performance versions of the Hillman Minx. During World War II, Kent were buying motorcycles including Matchless, AJS, Ariels and BSA. The first post-war cars in the fleet were Hillman Ten saloons.* Kent Constabulary

Middle Right: *Sir Percy Sillitoe (1888-1962), and one of Glasgow's police telephone boxes.* Alan Earnshaw Collection

Bottom Right: *As seen earlier, Stockport Borough Police favoured these American-inspired 2.6-litre Vauxhall Velox PASX models of 1960, but they also had examples of the earlier PAS and PASY models.* Vauxhall Motors

Top Left: *Centre stage in this atmospheric scene, one of Lancashire Constabulary's 1959 MG-As. It was mandatory for the drivers of these motorway patrol cars to be in possession of an advanced driving certificate.* Lancashire Constabulary

Middle Left: *Photographed in the 1960s at Longsight Police Station, Manchester, are a brace of Triumph TR4 models with Michelotti styling.* Alan D. Johnson Collection

Bottom Left: *High ranking officers of the Metropolitan police, Commander N Redford, and Superintendent R Butler inspect the squad's latest Sunbeam Tiger. These car's were produced between 1964 and 1967 as a high performance version of the Alpine that had originally been introduced in 1959.* Metropolitan police

Police forces of course were fiercely independent, and this was often reflected on the motor vehicles that were chosen before World War II, as there were really no set standards. The choice was often at the whim of the Chief Constable or the local authority's desire to patronise a local manufacturer. Thus it was possible to find almost Virtually every British marque (Scotland also had a very impressive motor industry at this time), thus served in a police force at some time during the years between the two wars.

When the 'Flying Squad' was formed as a rapid mobile response unit during 1918, this special branch of the police force was concerned with tackling serious crime such as armed robbery. Many other police forces followed the lead taken by London and formed their own Flying Squad sections. Accordingly, the cars allocated to these officers were the elite of the police motoring fleet, with such cars as Lea Francis, Invicta, Railton straight-eight and even Bentley having served as Flying Squad cars.

Large city and area forces had perhaps the greater justification for motorising their police force, but it was not really until the 1930s that the first patrol cars were to be seen on city streets for normal policing. For example, the West Riding Constabulary acquired their first piece of 'kit' in 1928, a brand new 9hp Standard patrol car. Meanwhile the City of London remarkably did not acquire its first two patrol cars until 1937. Their neighbours, the Metropolitan Police, had of course motorised much earlier and by the time Percy Sillitoe was introducing his scheme in Glasgow in 1933, the 'Met' already had 585 vehicles in use.

Unfortunately, as the fleet grew in size, so too did the number of accidents in which police were involved; in the first few months of 1934 the accident mileage ratio rose to one accident for every 8,000 miles. It could not be denied that a lack of experience and inadequate training facilities were a great handicap in raising the standard of driving. For these reasons the setting up of the Metropolitan Police Driving School at Hendon was ordered by the then Commissioner, Lord Trenchard in 1934. The first course for instructors was held in November 1934, and the first course for students began on 7th January 1935, when 21 young men signed on.

These were the forerunners of thousands, and they started with four weeks of instruction that included elementary motor mechanics and practical maintenance, in addition to driving. Eighteen instructional cars, including the Hillman 16, Ford 14 and Hillman 10hp touring cars were allocated to the school. For the purpose of general policing duties however, a wide variety of saloons and tourers were used.

Other police forces adopted a much more economical point of view, staying with motorcycles, three-wheelers (such as BSA and Morgan) or even small saloons built by Austin, Ford, Hillman, Jowett, and Morris etc. Some forces chose to utilise economical sports cars such as the Wolseley Hornet, whilst the Metropolitan Police and Reading Constabulary were among others who recognised the benefits of the MG-P series Midgets. These forces, along with the Oxford City Police and Warwickshire Constabulary. later progressed on to the well-loved T series models.

After World War II, some long established car manufacturers discontinued production and other marques merged with larger concerns, so the choice dropped in the 1950s. By this time Britain had its Big Seven manufacturers, Austin, Ford, Morris, Standard-Triumph, Rootes, Rover and Vauxhall, all these continued to supply a range of cars and commercial vehicles. Popular with many police forces, and particularly so with the 'Met' were the Wolseley 6/80 and the 6/90 models. Later choices were for the 6/99 and 6/110 models before this proud name was finally discarded by the BMC.

Riley were also a favourite with many police forces and many examples could be found of the beautiful Riley RMB and RMF models in police service. These were powered by a 2443cc four-cylinder engine and were really the last of the traditional Riley cars. Gloucestershire Constabulary purchased one for evaluation in 1946, and were so pleased with the example that, by the spring of the following year, no less than ten of these vehicle were in the fleet.

Top Right: *The Ford Zephyr Six, represented by this 1962 model, was probably one of the most widely used police cars during the early 1960s. Perhaps their greatest claim to fame was by way of television with them taking the starring role in the popular BBC television series* Z Cars. *West Yorkshire Constabulary*

Middle Right: *Although Ford cars were widely used throughout the world by both civilians and the police, the MkIV models of the Zephyr and Zodiac proved rather disappointing to some. Cars such as this 1966 Zephyr MkIV were tried by police forces, but they did not have the same functional appeal as previous versions.* West Yorkshire Constabulary

Bottom Right: *Landrovers were logical vehicles to have in rural police forces, for not only did they come into their own in severe weather, they were also ideal for towing mobile police stations for 'on-site' incident rooms. This one is a 1969 Series IIA, employed as a Motorway Unit in Yorkshire.* West Yorkshire Constabulary

Above: *This photograph clearly illustrates the eclectic vehicles that served the Dumfries & Galloway Constabulary in the early 1960s. Left to right the vehicles are a Morris J4 van, Landrover Series II, Austin A110 Westminster, Jaguar MkII, Ford Anglia, Austin A40 and a 1963 Morris Mini-van.* Dumfries & Galloway Constabulary

The Ford Motor Company was perhaps unique, in so much as from the Model T to the present day, they have remained at the forefront in the supply of police vehicles. Typical 1950s and '60s patrol cars from this manufacturer were such well-remembered icons as the Ford Pilot, and the Zephyr (MkI to MkIV), plus a smattering of 100E, 105E, Consul and Zodiac models. The Anglia 107E and 123E proved so popular during the 1960s that when Ford began to replace them with the new Escort models from 1968-onwards, they still offered a production line Panda car. Ford's principle rival in car production, Vauxhall, has also long been involved in the supply of police vehicles to many forces, so the marketing between the two (both of American parentage) has been very competitive.

Bedfordshire Constabulary in particular had long been a very devoted Vauxhall customer, as early as 1937 the Bedfordshire traffic division seemed to consist entirely of Luton-built cars, mainly Light Six, and the Twenty Five saloons. Other models that have entered police service in large numbers included the J series, the L series Velox and the later E series, which were followed by the F-type Victor and the PA-series Velox. In the 1960s, the HA Viva was widely used, followed by the HB Viva 'Panda Car'.

Among the other popular British police cars we find Humber, (including versions of the Super Snipe and Hawk models entering) many British fleets including the Metropolitan, Worcestershire and Blackpool forces. Various Hillman models also served with the police, including the popular Minx models from the pre-war MkII onwards, serving with such diverse forces as Somerset and the City of Salford; later on the Hillman Avenger took on the mantle of a Panda car. Talking of the Hillman Minx, its high performance stablemate, the Sunbeam Rapier was also chosen by some police forces, whilst the Singer SM1500 served in isolated cases.

Austin and Morris, who were merged to form the British Motor Corporation in 1951, both produced many examples of automobiles that were held in high esteem by the police. Among these was Cornwall, who were very impressed with their Austin A95 Westminster cars, other forces took the later A99 and A110 Westminster. As for Morris, Sheffield had a handful of the Morris 8 Series E models prior to and during World War II, which were maintained and driven by female crews. Later the Minor found almost universal appeal throughout the country in saloon, or van form, whilst Edinburgh even operated Traveller variants.

Jaguar cars were favoured by many police forces, and long before *Inspector Morse* came to our TV screens, this type of police car had already become famous throughout the medium of the film and television. Perhaps one of the earliest was the rather grand and stately MkV model, and among the forces that tried these were the Warwickshire and West Riding of Yorkshire Constabularies. These Jaguar models (built from 1949 to 1951) were available with a choice of either 2.5- or 3.5-litre six-cylinder engines. Remarkably handsome machines as they were, they were styled upon the pre-war models, and thus were superseded by the beautiful MkVII models during 1951.

The MkVII cars were rather a little too big for conventional patrol car work, they were 16' 5" long (10" more than the MkV model), but they were well-loved by police commissioners and other high ranking police officers as official staff cars. Examples of the MkVII served with police forces are to be readily found; Worcestershire, for instance bought two in 1952, with a further example following a little later in the decade. Incidentally, the MkVII cars were powered by the same 3442cc, six-cylinder engine that was designed for the superb Jaguar XK 120 sports cars that was introduced in 1949, a car that was to prove to be one of Jaguar's most popular models.

Top Right: *Rather an unusual choice for the vehicles of a police force are these Austin Mini Mokes. Merthyr Tydfil Borough Police used these during the 1960s.* South Wales Police Museum

Middle Right: *Here we see the two Hillman Imps (nicknamed Pinky and Perky) in the service of Dumbartonshire Constabulary. These vehicles were purchased from the Rootes plant at Linwood in Scotland to replace two motorcycles. The car registered GSN 840E is painted blue with a white bonnet, boot and doors, the companion car is in the opposite livery; both are finished with yellow roofs.* Courtesy Michael A. Scott

Bottom Right: *Here we see communications taking place between a police motorcyclist in the West Midlands and the driver of one of the Austin Mini-Cooper S models in 1968. These four-cylinder 1275cc-engined super mini cars had terrific manoeuvrability and a top speed of 97mph; but just imagine how difficult it would be for a burly bobby to get in and out of!* West Midlands Police

Top Left: *Like its neighbour Lancashire, the West Riding of Yorkshire force covered a wide and varied territory that ranged from heavily industrialised cities and towns to isolated rural areas. To cover this they used a varied fleet of cars, from high performance saloons to the Austin Minivan; as seen here with this 1967 example, which was part of a batch purchased to replace a fleet of 'Noddy Bikes'.* West Yorkshire Constabulary

Middle Left: *Looking every bit like a standard Triumph 2000, this car was a bit of a wolf in sheep's clothing, for YYG 427G, was actually one of the 2.5PI litre (petrol injection) models. When YYG 825G was taken out of service in 1971, it was purchased (with slight body damage) by my Editor Alan Earnshaw for £350. However, as the insurance group was so high, he could not afford to run it, so he quickly had it repaired and sold on, making a £75 profit on the deal.* West Yorkshire Constabulary

Bottom Left: *Illustrated here is another superb patrol car in the West Riding fleet. This was a Vauxhall Victor 3300 FD model. This is rather an early car as although the 1600 and 2000 models were introduced during 1967. The 3300 model was only introduced during 1968 when Vauxhall decided to fit the FD shell with the 3.3 -litre engine from the larger PC Cresta range. This car was painted in an unusual livery of pale primrose with the police signs on the flanks being dark blue and used on the M1 and M62 motorways.* West Yorkshire Constabulary

During 1955, Jaguar announced the more compact 2.4 and 3.4 saloons which, along with the improved MkII versions introduced in 1959, were what many police forces seemed to have been waiting for. Jaguar were now also producing a 3.8-litre engine, which gave a top speed of 125mph and a 0-60 time of just 8.5 seconds. To suggest that these new powerful Jaguars were to be found in every force would be an exaggeration, yet it would be easier to consider the forces that did not buy examples of these cars than the ones that did. They were ideal for high-speed cruising along the new motorways system, which truly began in 1959 when the first new 'super road' (not a by-pass) opened with the London-to-Birmingham motorway. This proved to be the start of a country-wide system, which was designed to link with the new system of 'super by-pass network' to relieve city centre congestion and improve road journey times.

As there were no speed restrictions on the motorways until 1965, many Chief Constables ordered their patrols to watch out for 'dangerous drivers'. As the local forces were ultimately given the responsibility of patrolling sections of motorways within their territory, they chose to up-date their fleet with cars especially for this role. Even the new E Type Jaguar was purchased for motorway work. The draw-back with cars of this calibre was their inability to carry much equipment, consequently performance saloons and estate cars became the norm.

Bedfordshire Constabulary used a mixture of the MkII and the earlier MkI Jaguar models side-by-side during the late-1950s and early-1960s, and the Metropolitan Police used them extensively too. Leicestershire & Rutland followed the lead set by Lancashire Constabulary, in that the examples of the MkII Jaguar that were delivered to the force during 1961 were painted white. Staffordshire Constabulary had several examples; of these, the batch that were delivered during 1965 had the white livery, but the six Jaguar 340 models that were purchased early in 1969 were finished in white with the high visibility 'Day-Glo' orange bonnets and boots. Other Jaguar models that proved very successful and favoured by the police were the S-Type, and also the XJ6,which was introduced during 1968.

Lancashire Constabulary had rather a long love affair with Ford cars. Using the range of Zephyr models, these were at one time the favoured steed for the motorway patrol boys in both saloon and Farnham Estate format. Also, the area had quite a sizable fleet of the MG-A sports car. Other types of cars that served and served well in this area of the country were the early E-series Vauxhall Velox saloon cars that were used as area cars during the 1950s.Worcestershire too were among the many forces to favour this model having six based at their new Hindlip Hall headquarters during the mid-1950s.

Top Right: *During 1968, nearly all the Austin Mini and BMC Minors that had been purchased by the West Riding of Yorkshire were re-painted in the 'Panda' scheme. That this picture is taken on the south side of Huddersfield can be confirmed by Victoria Tower (known locally as Castle Hill), which can be seen in the distance. This Austin Minivan (NWY 826E) was purchased in the same large batch as NWY 816E seen opposite in the old livery.* West Yorkshire Constabulary

Middle Right: *Many police forces chose the Triumph 2000 as an alternative to the Rover 2000 P6, which were introduced about the same time during 1963. They were very alike in many ways although the Triumph used a six-cylinder engine. This West Riding example was used on patrols along the A62 Trunk Road between Leeds and Huddersfield in the period prior to the opening of the M62.* West Yorkshire Constabulary

Bottom Right: *Jaguar cars introduced their XJ6 model with a 2.8 -litre engine during 1968. These proved to be very popular with the general car-buying public in this market. I know for a fact that West Riding of Yorkshire Constabulary had at least two of these superb cars, as I nearly got knocked down by one of the damned things when it was going at full tilt through Huddersfield. This September 1970 example dates beyond our 1950s and '60s period, but it illustrates the kind of cars that this force were using on the section of the M1 motorway as it ran north south through their 'patch'.* West Yorkshire Constabulary

Radio Control, by Alan Earnshaw

It may seem quite commonplace now, but we cannot under-estimate what a significant difference radio made to police work in the 1950s and 1960s. Therefore we cannot finish any overview of police work in this period without reference to how great this change was. Short-wave radio had obviously made massive improvements due to technology introduced in World War II, and its extension to use in the emergency services came as a natural progression once peace was resumed. With the increasing lawlessness (almost gangsterism) that came in the post-war era, captured so well in period by British motion pictures like *The Blue Lamp*, *Brighton Rock* and *Hell is a City*, every new technological aid became another tool for the police to use. Coupled with greater mobility and remote policing, radio communication became known as 'The Invisible Arm of the Law in Detection and Rescue Work'.

Above: *When Britain's first motorway opened at Preston in 1958, the local Police Authority had prepared well for the event, planning an excellent level of coverage all along the new by-pass. The main repeater mast being based in the 'space tower' of the services at Forton, the highest point on the entire stretch of six-lane road. It was administered by the control room at Preston, pictured here with the 'Plot' showing both fixed' radio transmitters and the position of mobile radio cars.* Lancashire County Constabulary

A series of excellent pictures showing radio cars at work in Lancashire in the early 1950s were discovered in the files of Vauxhall Motors, but there was little in the way of a narrative background to support these pictures. Fortunately, the radio work of a neighbouring force, Cumberland & Westmorland, was covered in a 1953 report in the local newspaper, the *Cumberland & Westmorland Herald*, which is so good as to be quoted verbatim.

Top Right: *The views on this page serve to show the improved communication systems employed by the police. Originally orders were given to the patrol car from headquarters, but when the officers wanted to report back they had to waste time locating a call box. When two-way radio phones were first experimented with, they improved things considerably. This unmarked 1947 Austin A40 Devon, in West Sussex, with its 'plain-clothes' crew would easily go unnoticed on the city streets.* West *Sussex Police*

Middle Right: *Although this method of* communication *seems positively archaic from today's point of view, this police-dog handler communicates with his headquarters via a 1954 Austin A40 Devon van as his alert companion patiently waits.* West Midlands Police

Bottom Right: *The 1966 MkIV Ford Zephyr, seen here shows radio policing 1960s-style, as an officer with Lancashire Constabulary, complete with a white-top for his cap, uses his Pye Westminster radio set. Sadly, these MIV cars were not as popular with police drivers as the previous MkIII models.* Lancashire Constabulary

"Have you ever wondered what happens when you dial 999? Of what steps the police have taken after you have reported some mishap-say, a road accident or an outbreak of fire? A *'Herald'* reporter who looked for the answer to those queries the other day found out that, so far as the counties of Cumbria and Westmorland are concerned, the whole business has taken on something of a 'new look'. Since March of this year police have been working with something more even than ever of their previous efficiency. That 'something' takes the form of the system whereby patrol cars covering the highways and by-ways of the two counties are connected to headquarters by short-wave radio.

Here is the means, which enables police aid to be on the scene of accidents within a time, which may be as short as two minutes. Here is the biggest 'bogey' haunting the freedom of any miscreant who sets foot in the area controlled by the Force.

Briefly the value of the new system lies in the speed with which it is now possible for the police to tackle their various tasks. For instance within minutes of a road accident being reported the nearest police car can be on its way to aid the injured. Or a car is reported missing, and almost immediately the patrolling policeman can be given a full description of it. Or it may be that the patrolmen spot a suspicious looking character. Particulars of the man are put through to headquarters and often though not in every case, needless to say – the description is found to fit a wanted man.

All reports and messages, orders and instructions, come and go through the information room, which forms part of the Force's new headquarters at Carlton Hall near Penrith. Here, in what was once the stately parlour of a private mansion, is the seven-days-a-week, 24-hours-a-day service, which acts as the 'brain' of the new system.

Above: *The image of the police force during the 1960s was of a highly efficient and organised operation, coupled with traditional service to the community. Becoming an immaculately dressed policeman with a highly polished Zephyr was the object of many schoolboy's dreams at the time.* West Yorkshire Constabulary

It is from the information room, that wireless contact is made with the various cars, but the success of the system does not depend merely on somebody 'calling all cars' from time to time. No less important is the giant map standing in the centre of the spacious room. About 110 square feet in area. It is actually a photographic enlargement and it provides a complete picture of mobile police activity in the two counties, with miniature vehicles, representing the patrol cars used by the Force, dotted hither and thither. Both map and models admirably suited to their purpose in every respect were made in the department of the Cumberland County Architect, Mr. J. H. Haughan.

The location of the patrol cars is checked by wireless at half-hourly intervals, and should an accident be reported, the sergeant on duty has merely to take a glance at the chart in order to decide which of the cars should be sent to take charge. The map serves a similar purpose should a car be reported stolen and subsequently be seen heading in a certain direction. Police cars in the vicinity are immediately alerted, with the result that many prompt arrests have been made.

A glance at the records kept in the information room, indeed, provides ample evidence of the manner in which stolen vehicles have been run to earth. A typical example is the story of the young Carlisle man who rounded off an evening's celebration by taking a joy ride in somebody else's car. From Carlisle, news of the car's disappearance was flashed to headquarters, and in turn; a description was at once sent out to the patrol cars. The result was that in little more than half-an-hour a patrolman on the main Penrith-Carlisle road spotted the car speeding south.

A chase ensued, and shortly after midnight only an hour after the receipt of the original message – the car had been overtaken (and the youthful joy-rider was anything but joyful). That was a pretty straightforward case. Others are more intricate and intriguing, requiring the diversion of police cars to cut off the missing vehicle, and it is upon the sergeant on duty – and his knowledge of the roads concerned – that the success of the operation is largely dependent. Miles from the hustle and bustle of the speeding cars, in the quietude of this room at Carlton Hall, it is immensely exciting to watch the progress of a big-scale chase as it is plotted out on the map.

Indeed, difficulty is sometimes experienced in getting some officers and other workers to go home – they want to see the excitement through to the finish! But the story told by the great chart is not always one of thrills on the broad highways. Sometimes the symbols spell death and disaster. To take a hypothetical case, three road or railway accidents in South Westmorland may be pinpointed, or in the hills surrounding Keswick a search may be in progress for a missing mountaineer. Again such incidents provide work for the police cars and for those on duty at headquarters, because the cars are often called on for use as what are known as 'incident posts'.

Direct from the scene of the occurrence, whatever form it may take, reports on the proceedings can be flashed to the information room, together with instructions as to any outside aid required. From remote spots, doctors, ambulances and rescue parties can be summoned in half the normal time. Ranking the importance with the wireless equipment and the large map, another feature of the information room is an extensive filing system. Escaped prisoners, wanted criminals, missing children, motorcars and other vehicles – details and descriptions of these are docketed away in orderly fashion, so that they can be consulted at a moments notice.

Like every other police station in the land, headquarters receive daily reports containing full descriptions of men wanted by the police. In the information room, these facts are methodically summarised on to tiny slips of card, which are then filed in alphabetical order, enabling a much quicker check to be made should any of the men be spotted by patrolmen. A similar system is employed in filing the registration numbers and descriptions of missing cars. By this means, many wanted men have lost their freedom when passing through the two counties. Take the case of a young man spotted for police questioning in the vicinity of Keswick. A subsequent check with headquarters revealed that the man's name was not on record - but the car he was driving was found to have been reported stolen from Southampton.

Or else the motor patrol may spot a car, the driver of which looks familiar-similar to a face the policeman has seen in one of the daily bulletins. He may be wrong of course, but he can always check with headquarters and find out wether anything is known about the car, which may give a clue to its driver's identity. Yes, there is more to the work of the motor patrol than looking for 'speeders', necessary as their job may be in the latter connection. It is a tribute to the alertness of the men that, with the aid of the files at headquarters,

they have arrested over a 100 wanted men since the introduction of the wireless system – men for whom no specific hunt was in progress, but who were merely spotted in the normal course of duty.

Sometimes it is a little, seemingly insignificant thing, which leads to a man's arrest. Indeed, a dented mudguard once resulted in the capture of a man who is now in prison on a charge of manslaughter. When the dent was first noticed at Kendal there was nothing to suggest that it was anything serious. Later, however, it was reported that a Lancashire man had been knocked down by a lorry, which had not stopped, sustaining injures from which he later died. Headquarters put two and two together, and the driver of the lorry was subsequently arrested at Penrith. Another example of the policeman's powers of observation was provided when the two counties' force received a private request to locate a motorist driving a car, registration number so and so, through the area. The motor patrols 'got their man', despite the fact that his number turned out to be somewhat different from the one quoted!

Transport drivers have already found the motor patrols a source of considerable assistance, and with the introduction of the wireless system, the benefits derived have increased considerably. Particularly is this so during the winter months, thanks to the way in which the new scheme of things have alleviated the problems caused by ice and snow on the roads. Patrol cars patrolling the main route of the A6 between England and Scotland where it crosses Shap Fell or the A66 across the Pennine mountains can keep headquarters informed as to the state of the road, and, should it become impassable, the staff on duty in the information room can immediately take whatever action they consider necessary.

Traffic diversions are speedily arranged – a facility, which is greatly appreciated by haulier's carrying urgently needed or perishable loads and up-to-the-minute bulletins are issued to the press, the BBC and others interested. In this way many lorry drivers are saved from the hardship of a chilly stay on top of Shap or Stainmore, waiting for the clearance of the roads. Some indication of the many uses to which the wireless cars can now be put is provided by these figures: in the ten months for which the information room has been in existence, over 55,000 messages have been sent and received.

That number includes 42,000 incidental messages-requests for the location of cars, reports on the state of the roads, etc. – and more than 13,000 operational messages in connection with accidents, manhunts, etc. In addition to the police cars, the messages go out to mixed receivers in the police stations at Penrith, Wigton, Carlisle and Kendal. In this way, each station is kept acquainted with the progress being made in connection with any incident, which may have occurred in the area it covers. This also has the benefit that any road-related incident that is likely to expand or move out of the area is covered. The police force that is more closely involved can immediately contact other police forces that may later also become involved in the incident thus giving them up to the minute detailed information.

Top Left: *This official photograph shows the telephone system employed during the early-1960s. This is obviously far removed from the compact mobile phones of today, but a two-way communication between the police station and the actual patrol car had only come into being some 30-years earlier; prior to this the patrol cars could only receive messages from the station and could not transmit back. The earliest cars equipped with two-way systems were operated by the Flying Squad, who often had the aerial replaced by a wire grid hung inside the roof of the car. Note will also be made of the seat belt style prior to the factory fitting of seat belts.*
Metropolitan Police courtesy A. D. Johnson Collection

Bottom Left: *Radio technicians who had been responsible for designing communication systems for the aircraft industry and the RAF had originally been approached by the police for similar miniature transmitters for police cars, and this in turn led to the introduction of systems like this two-way radio in this 1965 Vauxhall.* Vauxhall Motors

As already indicated, the messages are as varied as they are numerous. Fires, all manner of accidents, crime, trespass, domestic incidents or missing children, all receive speedy and efficient attention, while in an emergency, a constable has even been directed to attend to an expectant mother in the absence of a doctor or nurse. The baby was safely delivered! It is 'all in a days work' for the men and women of the motor patrols and those behind the scenes in the information room – an inconspicuous, and from the general public point of view, rather overlooked yet invaluable part of the Cumberland & Westmorland Police Force

One further aspect of the need and efficiency of the invaluable work of the radio communication systems was in the crucial area of liaising information when very slow and cumbersome loads were taken by road haulage; there was the great necessity for the police officers that were escorting the convoy to know beforehand the road conditions ahead. and if any obstructions were likely to occur along the way. Naturally on the obverse of this coin if a large load that was being transported by road way should suffer a breakdown then this could be kept to a minium inconvenience for other road users."

This report, with its now dated terminology provides an amazing look back to how police forces used radio half a century ago. Both police car radios and personal radios have become state-of-the-art pieces of high-tech equipment today, but we should not forget that at the start of the period covered by this book, law enforcement officers often had to make do with a stout pair of boots, or a bicycle, supported by a whistle and the ubiquitous blue police boxes. By the end of the 1960s, the blue police box had been more or less consigned to the pages of history, although one time traveller used a box to good effect. If only we could borrow *Dr. Who*'s TARDIS to travel back to the 1950s and '60s, we would see how great that change has been!

From the early days of police patrol car radio great advancements had been made by the end of 1969, in what was already an era of massive social change. Mobilised policing had moved on from the horse and motorbike to fast, high-powered road traffic patrol cars. The bobby on the beat had pushed his bicycle in to his garden shed and hung up his stiff hob-nailed boots, and could usually be found in the comfort of a pair of Doc Marten boots and a cosy Panda car. Mind you, life in a patrol car was not always the fun you might expect. I vividly recall sitting in the front of a West Riding 'dog patrol' mini van about 2am one winter's night in December 1969. After a long rescue search out on the moors, three of us were huddled and squashed in the front. The rain was pelting down in stair roads, we were all soaked to the skin and shivering so badly that we could not open the Thermos flask of Pea & Ham soup we had been given.

The dog-handler could have warned us that old Rex in the back had earlier eaten some of the Pea & Ham soup, and had developed a rapid case of flatulence. Believe you me, when it started, the cab of the Mini van was no place to be, even if it was a wild and violent night outside. As we stood outside, on the top of Holme Moss nearly 2,000 foot above sea level, I will swear to my dying day that damned dog was actually laughing at us as it looked out of the back windows. This of course was just one instance, other memories of sitting in police cars on the same moorlands bring back memories of more tragic incidents, including the search for the Moors Murders victims. However, we are sure that there must be many more amusing stories of police car life amongst our readers and as future police car volumes are planned in this series, we would dearly love to hear (via the editorial team) from officers who have served in this annul of transport history. To them, and the cars they drove, we are pleased to be able to recall the proud and efficient service to the entire British population by what many still regard as 'The Thin Blue Line'.

Top Right: *Here we have a trio of pictures showing the mobilisation of the force over the period covered by this publication. The fleet of Dorset Constabulary lined up in the top photograph shows a cross section of typical British cars with the majority of them being of the Ford Zephyr MkI models but also seen are examples of the Vauxhall Velox and Austin A90 Westminster, while in the back row an Austin A70 Hereford is a remainder of the earlier Austin marque.* Dorset Constabulary

Middle Right: *This is PC Geordie Calder, who progressed from a motorbike patrol to driving a 1960 MkII Ford Zephyr, with PTK 860 being his regular car. Note the loud-hailer, spotlight and chrome bell on the front bumper, whilst the white over-sleeve on his right side emphasises the long arm of the law.* Dorset Constabulary

Bottom Right: *Triumph introduced the first of their GT6 model during October 1966. These sports coupes were based on the Spitfire model but were of a fastback styling. The Triumph GT6 was actually powered by a tuned version of the 1998cc, six-cylinder engine that was fitted to the Triumph 2000 saloon cars. The GT6 was continued in production in series II and III form until 1973 with the most principle styling changes being to the radiator grille area.* Dorset Constabulary

Above: *New additions to the fleet of patrol cars that were operated by Sussex Constabulary in 1965 were these five Lotus Cortina models. Ford supplied the Cortina to the Lotus factory where they were fitted with high-performance engines, and lightweight alloy doors, bonnet and boot lids. Looking very little different from the conventional Ford Cortina MkI models that were in production at this time; except for the black radiator grille, the only real distinctive features were the bumpers, wheels and Lotus badges on the rear wings. These cars were capable of a tremendous performance and had a top speed of 106mph.* Ford Motors

This book, which was started by the late Alan Johnson (and who sadly died during 2002), has been an all too brief overview of some of the cars that have been operated by various police forces in Britain during the 1950 and '60s. The range of cars that have been used by police forces over these two decades was truly amazing, and it epitomised British motor manufacturing at its post-war zenith. Indeed, it represented the industry at its best, as only the best were considered for police service.

As we have seen, the advent of police call boxes, two-way radio, and fast patrol cars all helped the 'boys in blue' to fight a new generation of law-breaker that appeared in the 1950s and '60s, but it also served to remove the time-honoured bobby from his foot patrol and the day-to-day contact with the public. The subject is really far too interesting to merit this condensed small volume and really deserves to be told much more fully. However we have tried to illustrate some of the wide variety of vehicles that have served with many forces and we extend our sincere and grateful thanks to the many police forces who have contributed photographs.

The authors wish to extend their very grateful thanks to the many police forces who have assisted with this book by kindly submitting photographs and information, but especially to the Chief Constables (and their staff) who serve Devon & Cornwall, Dorset, Dumfries & Galloway, Greater Manchester, Lancashire, Sussex and West Yorkshire. They also would like to thank the British Transport Police, *The Cumberland & Westmorland Herald,* The Department of Transport, the University of Strathclyde, Ford of Gt. Britain, Jaguar Cars, Renault UK and Vauxhall Motors.